MICHIGAN:

State Legislators and Their Work

Gerald H. Stollman

**University Press
of America**™

Library of Congress No. 77-18633

ACKNOWLEDGMENTS

I would like to give special thanks to my wife Leila, without whom this book might never have reached culmination. Her assistance in typing, editing and encouraging my efforts enabled me to pursue my study to its conclusion.

I would also like to express my appreciation to Professor Rita W. Cooley of New York University. Dr. Cooley was instrumental in broadening the scope of this study, and her suggestions and guidance helped mould this work.

TABLE OF CONTENTS

TABLE OF CONTENTS

LIST OF TABLES

CHAPTER I

INTRODUCTION

"As citizens of the United States, we share in a precious inheritance -- the legislative form of government . . . This system of self-rule has given us the oldest continuous form of government now in existence."[1] Public attention has traditionally been focused on the national government and, not surprisingly, most academic research that is in existence has centered on this area of government. Despite an increased concern with state legislative systems by the academic community, state legislatures still do not receive the same amount of attention allotted to Congress. One scholar recently noted that in a ten-year period, four leading political science journals published 185 articles dealing with the legislative branch — 63% of which focused on Congress while the remainder discussed state legislatures.[2] Furthermore, an examination of doctoral dissertations completed during the same ten-year period indicated that 60% of these works dealt with Congress and 34% analyzed state assemblies.[3] The power and influence of the state legislatures in our system of government should not be underestimated. This fact may help to account for the recent increase in academic literature relating to the legislative system, particularly at the state level.

Like its counterpart in the national government, executive power in state government has grown at the expense of the lower chambers.[4] Commenting on this relationship between the legislative and executive branches, Jewell and Patterson have stated the following:

> The modern legislature may be more than ever subordinate to and dependent upon the executive, but it is nonetheless an important institution in a democratic political system. While the legislature is far less independent of the executive than it was in simpler times, legislative and executive activities are interdependent, and the legislature can check, frustrate, delay, reject and modify the policy extensions and inventions of the executive. What is perhaps more important, the legislature provides a critical connecting link between the people and the bureaucracy. Explanation of the linkage, of the functions of legislative systems and their instrumental activities, is a fundamental part of political science.[5]

In the years since the Second World War, more attention has been focused on state legislatures. Nevertheless, public knowledge regarding this aspect of government has remained meager.[6] State government, in general, arouses only a modicum of public interest among a state's own citizens.[7] When participants of a survey were asked to rank the types of public affairs they followed most closely, national political affairs were named as the most important, followed by local politics, international affairs and, lastly, state politics.[8] State legislatures are probably the least visible governmental institution, being privy to neither the national attention that Congress receives nor to the local attention focused upon city councils or boards of supervisors.[9] Generally, these legislatures meet infrequently — many for only a few months every other year. When they do meet, the public usually remains ignorant and/or indifferent to the deliberations and decisions.[10] The last decade has produced a number of changes which have helped the state legislatures to take their rightful place in government. Innovative policies and programs, reforms in procedure and structure, and an overall modernization have assisted in the legislative development. Further:

> This resurgence of state legislatures, and a renewed public interest in their role, have their roots in the reapportionment decisions of the Supreme Court in the mid-sixties. These rulings seemed to remove the most serious handicap under which state legislatures had labored for years: the growing disparity between the distribution of a state's population and the distribution of its legislative seats. For decades, state legislatures had been dominated by rural interests which constituted a diminishing minority of their population. In form and structure, moreover, state legislatures were geared to the pace and problems of an earlier, simpler America, not to the increasingly urgent and intricate needs of an urban, technology-oriented society.[11]

The changes which have taken place in the state legislatures have occurred primarily in recent years and have come about very gradually. Despite a significant increase in the number of published articles and books dealing with state legislatures, there is little which deals specifically with the Michigan State Legislature.[12] There is a wealth of information to be uncovered relative to Michigan's State Assembly. Hopefully, this legislative study will add to the aggregate of knowledge concerning state legislatures in general and the Michigan Legislature in particular.

The purpose of this book is to analyze the Michigan State Legislature in terms of the following categories: political culture, structure and organization, the legislators, the committee system, legislative leadership, Michigan's political parties, interest groups and policy outputs. An evaluation of this information is intended to dispel some of the ignorance concerning the State's legislative body, and to alter the popular notions of the members of the Legislature as lazy, underworked, capitalizing on their positions for personal comfort, e.g., junkets, and other such assumptions regarding the elected members of the Michigan Assembly.[13]

In researching the Michigan State Legislature, an eclectic approach was utilized. Constitutional, legal, historical, institutional, and behavioral methods of analysis were employed. The primary source material is derived from in-depth interviews taken from fifteen randomly 1971-72 legislators, out of a universe of 148 legislators from the 1971-72 legislative session. In addition, written questionnaires were sent to all members of the Legislature, with twenty-three responding. As Jewell and Patterson note in their classic study on legislative processes, "We cannot ignore legislative tradition, history, organization, and formal procedural rules because these are important factors in the behavior of legislators."[14] The research includes primary and secondary sources of information, in terms of interviews, correspondence, official state publications, newspaper accounts, relevant books, periodicals and journals. In order to accommodate the request of the legislators who were interviewed, in the case of direct quotations the legislator will not be named in the body of the dissertation. That is to say, all quotation sources will remain anonymous. Through the perceptions of the members of the Legislature and the writer's own observations, this work will attempt to describe the actual operation of the Michigan State Legislature. In so doing, it is hoped that many of the myths surrounding state government will be dissipated and that readers of this book will be enlightened in regard to the men and the machinery that enable Michigan's governing body to serve the citizens of the state.

The first category which is discussed in the paper is the political culture of Michigan. Essential to understanding the "whys" and "wherefores" of a state legislature, it is necessary to be aware of the political environment in which the legislature operates. "Wealth of the state's citizens is perhaps the most influential element of the environment."[15] Per capita and median family income are good predictors of state expenditure. The geographic and demographic characteristics of the state will play an important role in its economic and social affairs, as well as in determining the nature of political conflict.[16]

In order to better understand those individuals and groups which directly and indirectly influence the legislature, it is first necessary to comprehend the structure and organization of this law-making body. That is to say, we must know how each house is composed and how each operates. Much of this information lies within the Michigan Constitution. This document describes, in detail, the formal structure and organization of the Legislature. The informal, or actual, composition of the Assembly was ascertained through observation, interviews, and pertinent literature. The degree of restraint placed on the Legislature by the Constitution is also an important factor in the operation of the Legislature and the behavior of its members.[17]

3

The subject of power in Michigan's Legislature is also explored. In the national government, the key to power in the legislative branch rests with various committees. Whether the committee system plays a similar role in Michigan's Assembly or, if instead, party leaders or other individuals wield the powers of government — this question is examined. Other studies on state legislatures indicate that seniority, certain rules and restrictions — both formal and informal — and the number, size, and nature of the committees are all important factors in ascertaining where and with whom the powers of government lay.[18]

Once the subjects of political culture, structure and organization, and power in the Legislature have been discussed, this study proceeds to examine the individuals who carry out the law-making functions in Michigan's government. Such characteristics as socio-economic status, education, religion, and professional background are examined. Research that has been compiled previously appears to indicate that the typical American state legislator is male, white, Protestant, of Anglo-Saxon origin, and has the predominant occupation of either lawyer, businessman, or farmer.[19]

A discussion of the selection of legislative candidates will necessarily include the roles which political parties and interest groups play. At this point, however, the discussion of recruitment is concerned primarily with the factors that motivate citizens to seek to secure elective positions in Michigan's Legislature. Why a candidate runs for office will often affect his performance of his duties. The motives which have been explored in this work include: ambition, money, sense of civic duty, experience, frustration with the system, prestige, status, and the fun of the game.

The relationship between turnover and the seniority system is also examined.

> The record of turnover of state legislators suggests that returning to office is not particularly important to many of them. Thus, in many ways the state legislatures appear 'amateurish' in comparison with Congress, for example, where turnover is low and members acquire more parliamentary skills.[20]

Generally, there is a high turnover of state representatives. Most of this is voluntary. That is to say, the legislators do not seek re-election. There is evidence, however, which indicates a declining rate of turnover in the Michigan Legislature.[21]

Numerous factors influence the legislators in the performance of their duties. One area which is explored is the effect of bureaucracy on

4

the legislators. Barber has indicated that research facilities, secretarial assistance, office space, and salary may be important.[22] Thus, it would seem that the bureaucratic organization in the Legislature has an important effect on the legislators and the laws they pass. Further investigation will determine how efficiently the Legislature operates and if, in fact, the legislators are able to function as an effective check on the executive branch. The case load of the legislators is also examined. An overburdened legislator cannot function as well as a legislator with a light case load. In addition, a legislator cannot develop much expertise in a particular field if he must divide his efforts among several committees.

The political party is one element whose effects may be felt throughout the legislative system. The political parties in Michigan's Legislature could conceivably touch every aspect of the legislative process. The legislators were asked directly what role their party played in the Assembly, whether the parties are closely knit or loosely organized. A strong party will necessarily be more influential than a weak one. They were also asked to distinguish the parties from one another. One of the tasks of this study is to determine whether the party differences follow the traditional liberal/conservative lines or rather, stem from geographical or other factors.

Little is known regarding the legislators' campaign for office.[23] Regarding their first campaign for political office, the legislators were asked how they were recruited, how much help they received in their campaigns, the sources of their campaign assistance, the role of the party in recruiting the legislator and electing him to office, and the nature of the party's aid.

"'Interest group' refers to any group that, on the basis of one or more shared attitudes, makes certain claims upon other groups . . ."[24] This book is concerned with three aspects of interest groups: who they are, their affect on the election of legislators, and their role in the Legislature. Since the manufacturing of automobiles is a prime industry in Michigan, it is expected that the auto industry — namely, General Motors, Ford, and Chrysler — and various related organizations, such as the United Automobile Workers (UAW), the Teamsters, the American Federation of Labor (AFL), and the Congress of Industrial Organizations (CIO), will be influential interest groups in Michigan's government.[25] "One way to assess interest group activity is to ask state legislators what groups, if any, they perceive as being powerful in state politics."[26] This method should divulge the main interest groups and, perhaps, provide some indication of the extent of their activities.

The final category which is discussed concerns itself with the policy outputs of the Michigan Legislature. "The general legitimacy of the legislature as a decision-making system ultimately depends upon the character of its output."[27] An examination of the legislation that is passed by the Legislature and the manner in which a legislator arrives at his decision on whether to support or oppose a piece of legislation, including the criteria he employs, is useful in assessing legislative output. The political culture, parties, and interest groups of Michigan all have important effects on policy outputs. Yet another legislative output is the Legislature's oversight function with regard to executive administrative agencies. This section concludes the body of this study.

The following hypotheses are explored:

(1) The typical state legislator is male, white, Protestant, of Anglo-Saxon descent, and has the predominant profession of either lawyer, businessman, or farmer.

(2) Both political parties and interest groups play a significant role in the recruitment of legislative candidates and in the decision-making process in the Legislature. Thus:

    a. Both major political parties manifest a strong organization. The strength of party organization may be determined by the perceptions of the legislators themselves, by the regularity of party caucuses in the Legislature, or by partisan cohesion on important pieces of legislation, or by all of the above.

    b. These parties have definite and distinct ideologies based upon the traditional liberal/conservative philosophies.

    c. The major interest groups in the Legislature are the automotive industry and labor.

(3) There is a high rate of turnover in the Michigan Legislature. Consequently:

    a. Factors besides seniority play an important role in the selection of committee chairmen.

    b. Most of the important legislative assignments are carried out by only a few legislators.

    c. The Michigan Legislature has difficulty in attaining a high degree of expertise.

(4) Finally, although the Michigan legislators are well-staffed in comparison with other states, the legislative branch has a difficult time overseeing the executive agencies and, in fact, does not provide an effective check on the executive branch of Michigan's government.

"Before legislative analysis can effectively deal with problems of reform, indicate their probability of success, and predict their consequences, we shall probably need to learn a great deal more about legislative systems."[28] Hopefully, this work is a positive step toward an understanding of Michigan's legislative system and an addition to the aggregate of knowledge concerning legislatures in general.

---

[1] Citizens Conference on State Legislatures, **The Sometime Governments** (New York: Bantam Books, 1971), p. xi.

[2] Alan Rosenthal, **Legislative Performance of the States: Explorations of Committee Behavior** (New York: The Free Press, 1974), p. 5.

[3] Ibid.

[4] Duane Lockard, **The Politics of State and Local Government** (New York: MacMillan Company, 1969), pp. 257-8.

[5] M.E. Jewell and S.C. Patterson, **The Legislative Process in the United States** (New York: Random House, 1966), pp. v-vi.

[6] Ibid., p. vii.

[7] Kent M. Jennings and Harmon Zeigler, "The Salience of American State Politics," **American Political Science Review**, LXIV (June, 1970), p. 254.

[8] Ibid.

[9] Citizens Conference on State Legislatures, **op. cit.,** p. 2.

[10] Ibid., p. 3.

[11] Ibid.

[12] Robert W. Carr, **The Government of Michigan Under the 1964 Constitution** (Ann Arbor: University of Michigan Press, 1965), Floyd C. Fischer, **The·Government of Michigan** (Boston: Allyn and Bacon, Inc., 1965), and Ferris E. Lewis, **State and Local Government in Michigan** (5th ed.; Hillsdale, Michigan: Hillsdale Educational Publishers, 1968). Since Michigan's Constitution was revised in 1963, only these three works have been published which attempt to describe the state governmental system in Michigan. These publications all confine themselves mainly to the formal structural and organizational features of the Michigan Assembly. They explain how the system should operate theoretically, but not how it functions in fact. Furthermore, these publications relied largely on secondary source material. None were based on information gathered directly from legislative interviews.

[13] Frank Trippett, **The States: United They Fell** (New York: World Publishing Co., 1967), p. 3.

[14] M.E. Jewell and S.C. Patterson, **op. cit.,** p. 3.

[15] Herbert Jacob, "Dimensions of State Politics," **State Legislatures in American Politics,** ed. Alexander Heard (Englewood Cliffs, New Jersey: Prentice-Hall, Inc., 1966), p. 15.

[16] **Ibid.**

[17] Bell Zeller, **American State Legislatures** (New York: Thomas Y. Crowell Co., 1954), p. 16.

[18] John C. Wahlke, "Organization and Structure," **State Legislatures in American Politics,** ed. Alexander Heard (Englewood Cliffs, New Jersey: Prentice-Hall, Inc., 1966), pp. 128-142.

[19] William Keefe and Moris Ogul, **The American Legislative Process: Congress and the States** (Englewood Cliffs, New Jersey: Prentice-Hall, Inc., 1968), p. 137.

[20] Thomas R. Dye **Politics in States and Communities** (Englewood Cliffs, New Jersey: Prentice-Hall, Inc., 1969), p. 120.

[21] David Ray, "Membership Stability in Three State Legislatures: 1893-1969," **The American Political Science Review,** LXVIII (March, 1974), pp. 106-112.

[22] James D. Barber, **The Lawmakers: Recruitment and Adaptation to Legislative Life** (New Haven, Conn.: Yale University Press, 1965), p. 257.

[23] Jewell and Patterson, **op. cit.,** p. 530.

[24] David B. Truman, **The Governmental Process** (New York: Alfred A. Knopt, 1965), p. 33.

[25] Jacob, **op. cit.,** p. 27.

[26] Dye, **op. cit.,** p. 80.

[27] John C. Wahlke **et al. The Legislative System** (New York: John Wiley and Sons, 1962), p. 26.

[28] Jewell and Patterson, **op. cit.,** p. 525.

CHAPTER II

THE POLITICAL CULTURE OF MICHIGAN

Before it is possible to understand why a legislature functions in a particular manner, it is first necessary to comprehend the political environment of the state. The legislature is essentially a reflection of this environment. In support of this contention, Duane Lockard has stated: "There is every reason to believe that the existing political ethos of a state conditions the way a legislature functions as well as its legislative output."[1] An examination of past partisan conflicts is an important aid in gleaning information concerning the nature of the Michigan Assembly's political environment.

When, in 1835, Michigan ceased to be a territory and formally joined the Union, the two major political parties which evolved were the Democratic party and the Whig party.[2] The Democratic party stood for laissez faire liberalism.[3] The Democrats believed in separating law from morality, with fewer restraints placed upon individuals. They were perceived as the champions of egalitarianism and defenders against evangelical attempts to convert society to Christianity.[4] The Whig party, on the other hand, was highly moralistic and evangelical.[5] It favored the use of the government to influence moral and economic growth. The Whigs were nativistic, anti-Catholic, and inclined toward cultural homogeneity. During the 1830's and 1840's, the predominant issue separating the two parties was whether or not aliens should have the right to vote after two years of residency.[6] The Democrats were in favor of supporting this issue and, in fact, welcomed immigrants. The Whigs, however, were quite opposed to allowing aliens the right to vote.[7] During the period between 1835 and 1854, the Democrats lost control of the executive branch of Michigan's government only once. In 1839, a Whig named Woodbridge beat Farnsworth, the Democratic party's candidate for Governor.[8]

It was in the year 1854 that slavery became a salient political issue in Michigan. This issue led to the disintegration and eventual dissolution of both the Democratic and the Whig parties in the state. Simultaneously, it caused the birth of a new political party. Michigan's first Republican party convention assembled in Jackson, Michigan, on July 6, 1854. The predominant base of Republican support evolved from former Whigs.[9] The year 1854 marked the demise of Democratic party control of the executive branch of Michigan's government and the beginning of almost eighty years of Republican party domination throughout the state. This was the year of sweeping Republican victories, including the election of Kingsley S. Bingham, a former Democrat turned Republican, as Michigan's first Republican Governor.

By 1860, the Republican party had attracted a wealthier membership to its ranks than had the Democrats. The Republican party represented the business classes while the poorer classes were represented by the Democratic party. The most important conflict between the two parties was the ethnic cleavage.[10] The state's ethnic groups were disdainful of the Yankee, Protestant, middle class ethic of disciplined, moral, temperate conduct. The Catholic, Irish, German and French immigrants supported the Democratic party.[11] By the time the Civil War erupted, Michigan's Republican party was more of a Protestant party than the former Whigs had ever been.

By the 1920's the automotive industry had established itself as a prime source of Michigan's economic vitality. Thus, when the stock market crashed in 1929 Michigan was hit especially hard. Detroit produced five million cars in 1929; four years later production had fallen off by two million. While the effect of the Great Depression was devastating in most respects, it had a revitalizing effect on the Democratic party. In 1932 Michigan elected a Democratic Governor — the first since 1914.[12] Of even greater significance was the fact that the state legislature, for the first time in well over half a century, was dominated by Democrats.[13] However, Democratic control of that body was of a limited duration and by 1939, both chambers of the assembly were back under the firm control of the Republican party. The executive branch, however, was no longer a safe haven for Republican or Democratic candidates. Following the Depression the position of Governor became a politically competitive position. From the 1930's to 1948 the Governorship shifted from the Democrats to the Republicans on a fairly regular basis.

America's entry into the Second World War precipitated a large migration of unemployed workers all across the land to the industrial centers of the nation. There was a great influx of workers into Michigan, where the state's several defense plants provided employment for many. They came from the South and the agricultural Midwest, both black and white, in especially large numbers.[14] The Democratic party recruited many members from these newcomers and thus continued to grow after the Depression. In the years between 1948 and 1962 the Democrats maintained control over the executive branch but failed to dominate either house in the legislature. After 1962 the Democrats lost their hold on the Governorship when Republican George Romney was elected. Since Governor Romney took office, the Republican party has maintained its control of Michigan's executive branch of government.

When Romney was elected Governor, he became the first Republican to have captured that office since 1946. Yet his was not so much a Republican victory as a personal triumph for Romney the man, for not a single Republican candidate was able to win election to any of the state's administrative positions.[15] Put another way, the election of 1962 gave the Republican Governor a completely Democratic cabinet. Most of Romney's support came from the moderate wing of the Republican party, which was rooted primarily in the growing sub-urban areas.[16] The conservative Republicans from the rural areas were tepid toward Romney. After he was elected Governor this wing of his party became increasingly troublesome. He was never able to heal this rift between the suburban and rural factions of the Republican party. In 1964, Romney's coolness toward Barry Goldwater's candidacy for the Presidency branded him as a heretic with this conservative element. Despite President Johnson's landslide victory that year, Romney was re-elected as Governor with a 56% majority. However, he had to face the first Democratic-controlled legislature since the Depression. Two years later the Republicans regained control of the legislature, but since 1968 the Democrats have consistently held the majority in the lower chamber of the legislature and the upper chamber has been under Republican control by a very narrow margin — until 1974 when the Republicans lost their control of the Senate.[17] Since Romney's de-parture in 1968, his successor and former Lieutenant-Governor, William Milliken, has retained control of the Governor's office for the Republicans.

Today in Michigan, the principal source of Republican support emanates from a coalition of rural areas, small towns, businessmen in medium-sized cities and suburbs on Detroit's fringe.[18] In the past, the Michigan Manufacturers Association exercised considerable input over Republican party policy-making through its influence on Republican state legislators. To illustrate, Arthur Summerfield — a General Motors dealer in Flint and a past Postmaster General under the Eisenhower administration — was just one of a number of business leaders who were very influential in Michigan politics.[19] During the 1950's GOP policy reflected the ideals and interests of big business and the rural hinterland. Specifically, this policy favored low taxes, minimal govern-ment intervention and the protection of private property.[20] General Motors executives, as well as the leaders of the other automobile com-panies, helped in the formation of Republican party policies, used their influence to raise money, and sometimes staffed the party machinery.[21]

George Romney is an excellent example of an influential automotive executive. Prior to becoming Governor of Michigan from 1962-68, Romney was president of American Motors Corporation and exercised a good deal of political clout from that position. During an election General Motors would pressure those employees on the senior bonus roll — that is, those eligible for bonuses in addition to their salaries — to contribute to the Republican party in Michigan. In 1970, General Motors employees gave $2,000 to the Democratic party and between $100,000 and $200,000 to the Republicans.[22]

Detroit has been a bastion of Democratic party strength since the early nineteenth century and has consistently supported Democratic candidates.[23] Yet it was not until the Great Depression that the Democratic coalition evolved and it became recognizable as the Democratic party we know today. The Depression fostered a bipolarization of politics between the urban and rural areas, with Democratic party strength emanating from the heavily populated counties of the lower peninsula and the mining areas in the upper peninsula, while the rest of the state remained primarily Republican in its allegiance.[24]

The Democratic party's coalition is composed predominantly of labor, blacks, southern-born whites, Catholics and recent immigrants.[25] Since 1936 labor has been a potent force in Michigan politics.[26] When Democrat G. Mennen "Soapy" Williams campaigned for the Governor's office in 1948, he brought together two of Michigan's influential political groups and forged the labor-liberal alliance. The alliance enabled Williams to win an unprecedented six terms as Michigan's Governor. It was primarily the CIO-affiliated unions, and particularly the United Automobile Workers, that comprised the labor segment of this alliance.[27] In his 1948 election campaign, Williams had to overcome the opposition of both the Hoffa-led Teamsters Union and a Republican legislature which favored the Big Three automobile manufacturers rather than organized labor.[28]

Organized labor has made important contributions to the Democratic party in Michigan. It has helped to defray campaign expenses for those candidates it has supported. For example, in 1970 the UAW contributed $200,000 to the candidacy of Sander Levin, the Democratic challenger for the Governor's office.[29] The labor unions also have a large reservoir of people willing to run as county convention delegates. There was no need for the party to use patronage as an inducement for a union member to run for a political office because these individuals were compensated by their unions for time lost from the factories or from their positions as union officials.[30] Labor also has special caucuses at the Democratic state conventions. Since 1948, when the labor-liberal alliance was first formed, there has not been a state Democratic chairman elected who was unacceptable to labor.[31]

Michigan has been a strong two-party state since the Depression. Since 1920, the Republicans have successfully seized the Governorship 62% of the time, with the Democrats capturing the office the remaining 38% of the time. Since the 1964 reapportionment, the Democratic party has maintained control of the lower house of the Michigan legislature, with the exception of the 1967-1969 session. In the state senate, the parties were evenly divided from 1971 until 1974, when the Democrats gained a solid majority of twenty-four to fourteen.[32] Although the names of four or five different political parties usually appear on the ballot, Michigan is a two-party state. Since the 1930's the Republicans and Democrats generally attain about 98% of the vote.[33]

TABLE 1

GOVERNORS OF MICHIGAN FROM 1920 TO THE PRESENTa

Term of Office	Years Served	Governor	Democrat	Republican
1920-1926	6	Groesbeck		x
1926-1930	4	Green		x
1930-1932	2	Brucker		x
1932-1934	2	Comstock	x	
1934-1936	2	Fitzgerald		x
1936-1938	2	Murphy	x	
1938-1940	2	Fitzgerald		x
1940-1942	2	Van Wagoner	x	
1942-1946	4	Kelly		x
1946-1948	2	Sigler		x
1948-1960	12	Williams	x	
1960-1962	2	Swainson	x	
1962-1968	6	Romney		x
1968- ?	8	Milliken		x

a Statistics are taken from: State of Michigan, **Michigan Manual,** Department of Administration, 1971-1972, pp. 456-7.

The demographic characteristics of a state are important determinants on the nature of that state's legislative body. The magnitude of a state's populace may be a significant factor in the number of experienced representatives present in its legislature.[34] The greater the population of a state, the more numerous the experienced legislators will be in that state. According to the *1970 United States Census of Population*, published by the United States Department of Commerce, Bureau of the Census, Michigan's population numbers 8,875,083. It is the seventh largest state in the Union. In Michigan, 73.8% of the inhabitants reside in urban centers, while the remaining 26.2% dwell in rural areas. If we compare this statistic to 1900, when 39.3% of the population was urban and 60.7% was rural, it becomes obvious that this change in the distribution of Michigan's residents has had a considerable effect on the composition and policy outputs of the State Legislature.

The ethnic make-up of a state can have important ramifications with regard to the individual and partisan characteristics of its representative assembly. "Evidence indicates that legislators generally mirror their constituents in certain 'birthright' characteristics — race, religion, ethnic, and national background."[35] When Michigan became a state in 1837, its population numbered about 175,000.[36] At that time, the state's population had come primarily from New England and New York.[37] In addition, many Michigan residents were descendants of the French who had settled here at the beginning of the eighteenth century.[38]

During the decade of the 1840's there was large scale immigration to the state. This was due, in part, to the economic and political conditions in Europe.[39] Furthermore, Michigan actively encouraged and sought an increase in the number of new settlers. In 1845 the Michigan State Legislature made provision for the appointment of an agent whose duty was to prepare a pamphlet extolling Michigan's virtues and assets. Furthermore, it was to be the function of this agent to establish himself in New York in order to procure desirable new immigrants to settle in Michigan.[40] This pamphlet was published in both English and German and 5,000 copies were distributed throughout Europe by means of United States Consulates and various emigration associations. The Michigan Legislature repeated this action several times. In 1849, a pamphlet entitled *The Emigrants Guide to the State of Michigan* was published and over 7,000 copies were distributed at state expense. A commissioner of immigration was again provided for in 1859 and 1860. Michigan's program to attract immigrants was interrupted by the Civil War. It was resumed in 1870 and continued until 1885. By then Michigan had acquired sufficient new settlers to satisfy its population goal.[41]

The largest group to find its way to Michigan was the Irish.[42] Most were poor when they arrived. They settled in the cities where, it was believed, work could be found. The Irishmen proved themselves to be hard workers and labored at the construction of railroads and the digging of canals. In 1845, Ireland suffered the most severe potato famine in its history. This resulted in large masses of Irish leaving their native land to search for new beginnings abroad. Many settled in Michigan where there were abundant natural resources and an expanding economy.

The Germans were the second most substantial nationality to settle in Michigan. They located themselves primarily in Ann Arbor and the surrounding area.[43] Most of the German immigrants had been farmers and came to Michigan with sufficient money to buy their own land and continue their profession in their new home. A further influx of German immigrants into the Wolverine state occurred in 1848, when an unsuccessful revolution caused many intellectuals to flee their homeland.

The Dutch immigrants arrived in Michigan in 1846.[44] They settled in Grand Rapids, Grand Haven, Muskegon, Kalamazoo, and an area which eventually became Holland, Michigan.[45] The Dutch population has remained in these northern lower peninsula cities, perpetuating their ethnic traditions. For example, the Dutch of Holland, Michigan, present a large-scale tulip festival every spring, just as their European counterparts have done every year for generations.

The next major migrant wave followed closely on the heels of World War One. Canadians were the largest nationality to flow steadily into Michigan in the years after the conclusion of the War. Immigration from eastern European countries — Poland, Russia, the Ukraine and Czechoslovakia — also brought new residents to Michigan in great numbers. These groups established themselves principally in Detroit. In the upper peninsula of Michigan, immigrants from the Scandinavian nations evolved into the dominant ethnic group.[46]

Another major migration that has had significant political ramifications is the exodus of blacks from the southern United States into Michigan. In 1900 the blacks totaled 15,816 or less than 1% of Michigan's inhabitants.[47] As Bald further states in his book *Michigan in Four Centuries,* twenty years later the Negro population had quadrupled to 60,082. However, this still represented only 1½% of Michigan's total. Between 1920 and 1930 another large increase in blacks occurred, giving the black population a total of 169,453 members and constituting 3% of the state's total population. The Second World War and the concurrent availability of jobs in Michigan's various war plants attracted even more Negroes to the state. From 1940 to 1950 the black population increased from 216,463 to 452,000 — 7% of the total population in the state. At the last census in 1970, it was found that the number of blacks living in Michigan had increased to 991,000, or 11% of Michigan's total population.[48] This was a 38% increase in a period of ten years, within the black populace.[49]

Two-thirds of the state's black population lives in the city of Detroit and represents 44.5% of that city's population, according to the 1970 census. While most of Michigan, and especially Detroit's suburbs, have experienced a numerical growth in population, the city of Detroit went from 1,670,144 in 1960 to 1,511,482 in 1970 — a very definite decline.[50] Although this decrease in Detroit's population, as a whole, has transpired in recent years, the city's black residents have continued to increase their number. Regrettably, the rapid increase in the black population has been a serious source of tension. The race riots in 1943 and 1967 bear witness to this fact. Racial problems remain a salient political issue in Michigan.[51] Race-related issues such as cross-district busing have had deep national impact. Governor George Wallace was able to capitalize on that particular issue during the Presidential Primary in Michigan in 1972, when he received 51% of the total votes cast.[52] In that primary, Wallace made busing his number one issue, with obvious success.[53] The blacks of Michigan are an important source of Democratic party strength. An indication of their importance is reflected in the Michigan State Legislature, where the two black Senators and all nine black members of the House of Representatives belong to the Democratic party.[54]

At this point, it might prove helpful to summarize some of Michigan's basic demographic features. The information which follows is based on the *1970 United States Census of Population.* Foreign stock, i.e., immigrants and first generation Americans, make up 19% of Michigan's population. Racially, whites number 7,833,474 and represent 88% and blacks number just under one million and comprise 11% of the state's populace. Catholics make up 26.8% of the population and 1.1% is Jewish. The various percentages of those Michiganders who are employed is distributed thusly: white-collar workers, 44.9; blue-collar workers, 40.7; service workers, 12.9; and farm workers, 1.5. The median family income in 1970 was $11,032. The median number of school years completed is 12.1. The major industries in Michigan are: manufacturing, e.g., automobiles and furniture; tourism; and agriculture, e.g., dairy farming and cereal production.

"A line drawn horizontally across the lower peninsula from Lake Michigan to just below the tip of Saginaw Bay and including within it the northern border of Muskegon County and the south-ern border of Bay County is the traditional division between industrial and agricultural lower Michigan and upper Michigan."[55] This geographical cleavage is thought to have considerable impact on the policy outputs of a legislature, for according to some authorities, rural/urban conflicts are the most important sources of dissension in a state legislature.[56]

As previously cited, 26.2% of Michigan's population lives in rural areas, which would include farms, small towns, and villages. About 250,000 residents are employed in agriculture-related industries.[57] These citizens represent the backbone of the Republican party in Michigan.[58] The great majority of Michigan's rural population is clustered in the southern half of the lower peninsula where the soil is most fertile. Increased growth of urban-industrial centers has been at the expense of the farm population.[59] The upper peninsula and the northern half of the lower peninsula have vast expanses of wooded hills, lakes, and resorts. These natural assets have given rise to the develop-ment of Michigan's second largest industry — tourism.[60] At the same time, these are areas with poor soil, depleted mines, and relatively few inhabitants — only 6% of the state's total population.[61]

The southern half of Michigan's lower peninsula is essentially the state's industrial home. The major industrial centers are: Flint, Detroit, Lansing, Grand Rapids, and Muskegon. Detroit remains the automobile capital of the United States with General Motors, Ford, Chrysler, and the American Motors Corporation all having their world headquarters situated in the city.[62] The automotive industry has fostered the development and growth of one of the most powerful and influential labor movements in the nation. The United Automobile Workers, or UAW, is the principal union of automotive and farm implement workers in Michigan and elsewhere.[63] Its importance is reflected in the state's politics.

The political traditions and styles of a state will also affect the government of that state, particularly regarding its legislative outputs. Very early in the state's history the government of Michigan was involved in positive programs, which included the building of roads, canals, and railroads. Unfortunately, the state almost went bankrupt from borrowing funds for these internal improvements. The legislature was held responsible for the financial difficulties, and as a result, the constitutional convention of 1850 substantially reduced its legislative powers. To some degree, this distrust is still reflected in Michigan's present constitution. For example, the legislature is specifically forbidden to impose a graduated income tax on the citizens of Michigan.[64]

Issues have almost always played a dominant role in the politics of Michigan. Back in the 1850's, slavery was a salient issue. There was a good deal of abolitionist sentiment in Michigan, most of it centered in various church groups and in the Republican party. Detroit was also a part of the underground railroad. For this reason, Michigan was subject to constant raids by various slave owners who were attempting to recapture their former slaves. These intermittent forays resulted in the forging of strong anti-slavery sentiment in Michigan.[65] When the Civil War broke out the residents of Michigan supported the Union cause enthusiastically.[66] The conclusion of the war put an end to slavery as a major issue in Michigan politics.

From about 1890 until the early 1920's, Michigan was under the influence of the Progressive movement. In this state the movement was personified by Hazen S. Pingree, the Republican mayor of Detroit from 1890 to 1896, and a Governor of Michigan from 1896 until 1900. He was a reform mayor. Pingree was especially effective in his battle against corrupt utility companies who were overcharging the city for their services. Pingree was a retired businessman, but because of his zealous fight against the utility companies, along with various other reforms, he was considered to be a traitor to his class. As Governor of Michigan, Pingree crusaded for greater citizen participation in government. He advocated such reforms as the initiative, the referendum, direct primaries for nominating state and local officers, recall of elected officials, and the direct election of United States Senators.[67] He was not a strong party man, and when William McKinley campaigned for the Presidency, he received practically no support from Pingree. Many of the reforms that Pingree fought for did not materialize until after his term of office expired. Some of these reforms were incorporated in Michigan's third constitution in 1908 — for example, direct primaries.

Interest groups played an important role in the reform movement of the late nineteenth century. One group which was particularly effective was the Knights of Labor.[68] To a large extent, the Knights of Labor represented the labor movement in the state at this time. The organization had branches in Detroit, Saginaw, and Bay City. In 1886, they were responsible for electing thirty-eight members to the state legislature. Their lobbying helped advance the enactment of laws providing for compulsory school attendance, the requirement of safety devices in factories, the inspection of mines, and very significant child labor laws.[69] They promoted legislation which prohibited the employment of children under the age of ten years, and the employment of any individual under age eighteen was limited to no more than ten hours per day and sixty hours a week. Another significant interest group in Michigan at this same time was the Patrons of Husbandry, popularly known as the Grange.[70] This group battled primarily for the reform of railroad rates and other issues that were in their interest.

By the 1920's, the reform movement had spent itself and was followed by a period of reaction and lawlessness, especially in the city of Detroit where rum-running was prevalent during the Prohibition era. This was a time period which gave rise to murderous gangs, such as the Purple Gang, the River Gang, and the West Side Gang.[71]

The Depression revitalized politics in Michigan. The rise of the UAW-CIO breathed new life into the Democratic party. This union placed its major emphasis on programmatic politics.[72] The consequence of these factors, i.e., the Depression and the rise of union membership, was to make both political parties more attentive to issues.[73] In 1940, the merit system was introduced in the administrative agencies. Today, it is mainly the Secretary of State's office and the Highway Department which retain lucrative patronage positions at the state level. The two major interest groups which have traditionally comprised an important segment of the Republican party — the Automobile Manufacturers — and the Democratic party — labor — are not in the political arena for the usual prizes — i.e., appointment to positions and the awarding of contracts. These groups are more interested in controlling the social and economic policies of the state government.[74] Governor Williams, who was strongly endorsed by labor, and Governor Romney, who received strong support from big business, had one basic similarity — both emphasized programmatic politics. They both believed in an active government. "Michigan politics continues to be issue rather than patronage oriented, with a strong civil service remaining as a barrier to a spoils system."[75]

To comprehend fully the political environment in which Michigan's state government operates, it is helpful to define and examine its political culture. To some degree, this examination has been detailed in the preceding pages. It remains, then, to properly define political culture and apply this definition specifically to the state of Michigan. According to Daniel Elazar, political culture is defined as "the particular pattern of orientation to political action in which each political system is embedded. Political culture, like all culture, is rooted in the cummulative historical experiences of particular groups of people."[76] It is this definition which will be utilized to further assess the nature of Michigan's political milieu.

Elazar has divided political culture into three basic categories which he calls individualistic, moralistic, and traditionalistic.[77] The individualistic culture emphasizes the democratic order as a market place. This culture stresses a limitation on government intervention. Politics is perceived as a business, a matter of mutual obligation rooted in personal relationships. It encourages a party system that is competitive and is based on patronage. The traditionalistic culture reflects a pre-commercial concept of politics. It views society as hierarchical; in other words, this culture is based on a class system. It accepts government as a positive force in the community. The government is run by a relatively small and self-perpetuating elite. This group inherits its right to govern through family and social ties. The traditionalistic culture is usually represented by a one-party state and is anti-bureaucratic. The third category in Elazar's theory is the moralistic culture. In the moralistic political culture, politics is perceived as being in search of the good society. Good government is measured by the degree to which it promotes the public good in terms of honesty, selflessness, and commitment to the public welfare. Issues play an important role in a moralistic political culture. Party regularity is not of prime importance. Greater emphasis is placed upon amateur participation. As in the individualistic political culture, the moralistic culture also stresses competitive party politics. Unlike the traditionalistic political culture, the moralistic culture encourages a bureaucratic system of government. It is interesting to note that the moralistic political culture is a product of puritan New England, and has been reinforced by North Sea and Jewish ethnic groups.[78] This culture is most evident where Yankee, Scottish, Dutch, Scandinavian, and Swiss heritages are dominant.[79]

In a related study, Ira Sharkansky devised a culture scale based on Elazar's three categories.[80] Sharkansky utilized certain predictors, such as voter turnout, the liberlization of suffrage requirements, tax effort, expenditures and measures of services in the fields of education and public welfare. The resultant scale ranges from 1.0 (most moralistic) to 9.0 (most traditionalistic).[81] Michigan ranks 2.0 on Sharkansky's scale. Accordingly, to a large extent Michigan's political culture can be described as Moralistic.[82] In fact, in Elazar's most recent edition, he cites the dominant political culture in Michigan as moralistic.[83]

This, then, concludes a description of the political environment surrounding the Michigan State Legislature. This background should enhance the understanding of the legislature and its environment — an essential element to an understanding of the legislature's function in the state. No public insititution, including government, operates in a vacuum. It behaves as it does as a result of the various forces working upon it — both past and present, from both within and without.

---

[1] Duane Lockard, "The State Legislator," **State Legislatures in American Politics,** ed. Alexander Heard (Englewood Cliffs, New Jersey: Prentice-Hall, Inc., 1966), p. 99.

[2] State of Michigan, **Michigan Manual,** The Department of Administration, 1971-1972, p. 454.

[3] Ronald P. Formisano, **The Birth of Mass Political Parties: Michigan, 1827-1861** (Princeton, New Jersey: Princeton University Press, 1971), p. 109.

[4] **Ibid.,** p. 329.

[5] **Ibid.,** p. 109.

[6] **Ibid.,** p. 81.

[7] **Ibid.,** p. 89.

[8] State of Michigan, **op. cit.,** 1971-1972, p. 454.

[9] F. Clever Bald, **Michigan in Four Centuries** (New York: Harper and Brothers Publishers, 1954), p. 258.

[10] Formisano, **op. cit.,** p. 301.

[11] **Ibid.,** p. 303.

[12] State of Michigan, **op. cit.,** p.. 456.

[13] **Ibid.,** pp. 97-99.

[14] Stephen B. and Vera H. Sarasohn, **Political Party Patterns in Michigan** (Detroit: Wayne State University Press, 1957), p. 3.

[15] Richard C. Fuller, **George Romney of Michigan** (New York: Vantage Press, 1966), p. 76.

[16] Albert L. Sturm, **Constitution-Making in Michigan, 1961-62** (Ann Arbor, Michigan: Institute of Public Administration, University of Michigan, 1963), p. 107.

[17] State of Michigan, **op. cit.,** pp. 97-99.

[18] William J. Keefe, "The Functions of Powers of the State Legislature," **The American Legilsative Process: Congress and the State,** ed. Alexander Heard (Englewood Cliffs, New Jersey: Prentice-Hall Inc., 1968), p. 42.

[19] Neal R. Peirce, **The Megastates of America** (New York? W.W. Norton and Co., Inc., 1972), p. 406.

[20] **Ibid.**

[21] Carolyn Stieber, **The Politics of Change in Michigan** (Lansing, Michigan: Michigan State University Press, 1970), p. 8.

[22] Neal R. Peirce, **op. cit.,** p. 407.

[23] F. Clever Bald, **op. cit.,** p. 326.

[24] Stephen B. and Vera H. Sarasohn, **op. cit.,** p. 25.

[25] Robert Lee Sawyer, **The Democratic State Central Committee in Michigan, 1949-1959: Rise of the New Politics and the New Political Leadership** (Ann Arbor, Michigan: Institute of Public Administration, 1960), p. 243.

[26] **Ibid.,** p. 7.

[27] Edward W. Chester, **Issues and Responses in State Political Experience** (New Jersey: Littlefield, Adams and Co., 1968), p. 59.

[28] **Ibid.,** p. 61.

[29] James M. Hare, **With Malice Toward None** (Lansing: Michigan State University Press, 1972), p. 19. The author served as Michigan's Secretary of State from 1955 to 1970.

[30] Stephen B. and Vera H. Sarasohn, **op. cit.,** p. 22.

[31] James M. Hare, **op. cit.,** p. 19.

[32] State of Michigan, **Michigan Manual,** Department of Administration, 1973-1974, pp. 99-100.

[33] Joseph LaPalombara, **Guide to Michigan Politics** (East Lansing, Michigan: Michigan State University Press, 1960), p. 22.

[34] Belle Zeller, **American State Legislatures** (New York: Thomas Y. Crowell Co., 1954), p. 69.

[35] Thomas R. Dye, **Politics in States and Communities** Englewood Cliffs, New Jersey: Prentice-Hall Inc., 1969), p. 117.

[36] F. Clever Bald, **op. cit.,** p. 205.

[37] **Ibid.**

[38] State of Michigan, **op. cit.,** p. 2.

[39] F. Clever Bald, **op. cit.,** p. 262.

[40] **Ibid.**

[41] **Ibid.**

[42] **Ibid.,** p. 258.

[43] **Ibid.,** p. 260.

[44] **Ibid.,** p. 261.

[45] **Ibid.**

[46] **Ibid.,** p. 395.

[47] **Ibid.**

[48] **1970 U.S. Census of Population,** U.S. Department of Commerce, Bureau of the Census, p. 24-56.

[49] **Ibid.**

[50] **Ibid.**

[51] Carolyn Steiber, **op. cit.,** p. 93.

[52] "Campaign 72: Michigan Presidential Primary," **Congressional Quarterly,** XXX, No. 19 (May 6, 1972) p. 1032.

[53] "Michigan Primary Results," **Congressional Quarterly,** XXX, No. 21 (May 20, 1972), p. 1139.

[54] State of Michigan, **op. cit.,** pp. 179-217.

[55] Stephen B. and Vera H. Sarasohn, **op. cit.,** p. 1.

[56] Thomas R. Dye, **op. cit.,** p. 125.

[57] "Michigan," **Encyclopaedia Britannica,** 14th ed., Vol. XV (1968), 373.

[58] Joseph LaPalombara, **op. cit.,** p. 10.

[59] **Ibid.**

[60] "Michigan," **Encyclopaedia Britannica,** 15th ed., Macropaedia Vol. XII (1974), 107.

[61] Neal R. Peirce, **op. cit.,** p. 403.

[62] **Ibid.,** p. 413.

[63] **Ibid.**

[64] Michigan, **Constitution,** Art. 9, sec. 7.

[65] F. Clever Bald, **op. cit.,** p. 261.

[66] **Ibid.**

[67] **Ibid.,** p. 330.

[68] **Ibid.,** p. 296.

[69] **Ibid.**

[70] **Ibid.,** p. 303.

[71] **Ibid.,** p. 385.

[72] Robert Lee Sawyer, **op. cit.,** p. 261.

[73] Kenneth T. Palmer, **State Politics in the United States** (New York: St. Martin's Press, 1972), p. 50.

[74] Stephen B. and Vera H. Sarasohn, **op. cit.,** p. 69.

[75] Carolyn Stieber, **op. cit.,** p. 112.

[76] Daniel Elazar, **American Federalism: A View From the States** (New York: Thomas Y. Crowell Co., 1966), p. 84.

[77] **Ibid.,** p. 86.

[78] Daniel J. Elazar, **Cities of the Prarie: The Metropolitan Frontier and American Politics** (New York: Basic Books, Inc., 1970), p. 264.

[79] **Ibid.**

[80] Ira Sharkansky, "The Utility of Elazar's Political Culture: A Research Note," **Polity 2,** (Fall, 1969), p. 81.

[81] **Ibid.**

[82] **Ibid.**

[83] Daniel J. Elazar, **American Federalism: A View From the States** (2d ed.; New York: Thomas Y. Crowell Co., 1972), pp. 117-8.

CHAPTER III

A GENERAL VIEW OF MICHIGAN'S LEGISLATURE

Included in the 1963 Michigan constitution are many articles relating specifically to the legislature. The constitution has accorded the legislative body many powers. These include the following: the power to levy taxes and appropriate funds for the operation of the state (Art. IX, Sec. 1); the ability to regulate the activities of the state's political parties and the elections (Art. II, Secs. 1-7); the authority to control the police power which regulates and guarantees the civil rights of the citizens of Michigan (Art. I); the power to oversee the ownership and use of property (Art. X, Secs. 1-6); the ability to pass regulations regarding the validity of contracts and the power to regulate various professions, including the establishment of basic laws regarding the licensing of various professional groups, including teachers, dentists, lawyers, doctors, etc.[1]

The constitution further stipulates the organization of the Michigan State Legislature and outlines the election and privileges of the legislators.[2] Michigan's assembly is bicameral. The upper chamber, or Senate, consists of thirty-eight members. The lower chamber, or House of Representatives, is comprised of one hundred and ten members. The Senators are elected for four-year terms, whereas the Representatives' term of office is two years. These elections are held on the first Tuesday after the first Monday in the month of November, biennially, in even-numbered years, concurrent with Congressional elections. Members of the legislature are nominated by popular vote of their respective parties in primary elections held in August of an election year. The legislators meet in the State Capitol building in Lansing on the second Wednesday in January and remain in session as long as they deem necessary. All members of the legislature are exempted from civil arrest and civil process during the time the legislature is in session, as well as the five days preceding and the five days succeeding the legislative session. According to Section 11 of Article IV of Michigan's constitution, the legislators are entitled to unlimited free speech on the floor of their chambers and are immune from prosecution for any speech in either house. Section 14 of this Article states: "a majority of the members elected to and serving in each house shall constitute a quorum to do business."[3] Absent members may be compelled to attend meetings. Neither house may adjourn for a period in excess of two days without the consent of the other house.

Once the new session commences, the first task of the members is to organize their respective houses. Each party holds a caucus and elects its leadership. At this time, the party caucus will also determine which legislators will sit on what committee or committees. Each chamber has the right to choose its own officers and to determine the rules and procedures that will be followed in the respective houses, according to Article IV, Section 16. This Article further states: "Each house shall be the sole judge of the qualifications, elections and returns of its members, and may, with the concurrence of two-thirds of all the members elected thereto and serving therein, expel a member."[4] A journal is kept in both the Senate and the House so that all proceedings may be recorded and published. These journals are available for public inspection.

The members of the Senate come up for election every four years, at the same election as that for governor. In Michigan, each Senate district consists of 233,753 individuals, on the average.[5] In order to be eligible to serve as a member of the Michigan Senate, one must be a citizen of the United States and be at least twenty-one years of age. He must live in the district he seeks to represent and, if he should move during his term of office, he must vacate his elected seat. Article IV, Section 7 further stipulates that: "No person who has been convicted of subversion or who has within the preceding 20 years been convicted of a felony involving a breach of public trust shall be eligible for either house of the legislature."[6]

The lieutenant governor presides over the Senate meetings as president of that body. When an equally divided vote arises in the Senate, the lieutenant governor may cast his vote in order to break the tie. When he is absent from the Senate, his position is filled by the president pro tempore. The president pro tempore is selected by his fellow Senators. His is largely an honorary position.

There are eighteen standing committees in the Senate.[7] The most important committees, according to the legislators themselves, are: Appropriations, Education, Judiciary, and Taxation and Veterans' Affairs. These committees have a minimum of five Senators sitting on each of them.[8] The largest of the committees, which is the Appropriations Committee, has ten members.[9] Most of the Senators serve on three committees. However, Senators serving on the Appropriations Committee rarely serve on any additional committees, and never more than two.[10] Finally, it is the Senate which approves most of the administrative appointments that are made by the governor.

Turning now to the lower chamber of the Michigan State Legislature, the House of Representatives, the constitution stipulates that: "the house of representatives [sic] shall consist of 110 members elected for two-year terms from single member districts apportioned on a basis of population. . . "[11] The size of such a district numbers 80,751 inhabitants on the average.[12] The qualifications of members elected to the House of Representatives are the same as those which apply to Senate members. Representatives are nominated in the regular August primary for election to two-year terms. There are thirty-three standing committees in the House.[13] The average committee consists of 10.7 members, with the smallest committee, Youth and Student Participation, having seven members and the Appropriations Committee, which is the largest committee in the House, being comprised of 17 members.[14] Most members serve on approximately four different standing committees.[15] Representatives who serve on the House Appropriations Committee do not serve on more than one other committee. The most important standing committee in the House — again, according to the legislators themselves — is Appropriations, with the Judiciary, State Affairs, and Taxation committees also considered to be of particular importance.

An important office that has been placed under the purview of the Michigan State Legislature is that of the auditor general. Article IV, Section 53 is concerned with this office and details the appointment, qualifications, term of office, removal from office, and function of the auditor general. He is appointed by a majority vote of both houses of the legislature and is responsible to the legislative body. His principal responsibility is to see that the state's monies are spent in accordance with the provisions of the legislature. One legislator describes the duties of the auditor general thusly: "His job is to audit cities, counties, legislatures, colleges, univesities, . . . everybody! And to see to it that they're using the proper accounting procedures and that they're spending their money efficiently." The auditor general must be a certified public account licensed to practice in Michigan. His term of office is eight years. He can be removed from office for cause by a two-thirds vote of both houses. The auditor may, when directed by the legislature, employ independent accounting firms or legal counsel to assist him with his audits. He must report annually to the legislature and to the governor, and at other times as requested by the legislature.

The major occupations of the members of Michigan's assembly are law, teaching, and business.[16] In the state Senate in 1972, 29% of the membership were lawyers, 19% were teachers, and 16% were businessmen. In the lower chamber in that same year, 21% were lawyers, 17%

were businessmen, and 10% were in the teaching profession. In comparing this occupational breakdown with the same legislature just ten years earlier, i.e., 1962, there is one noteworthy difference — farmers had much greater representation in the 1962 legislature.[17] In the state Senate that year, 29% of the members were attorneys, 24% were businessmen, 12% were farmers, and there were no teachers. In the state House of Representatives in 1962, 8% were lawyers, 23% were businessmen, 19% were farmers, and 2% were teachers.

In a study conducted over thirty-five years ago, Charles Hyneman noted the predominance of lawyers in the membership of state legislatures throughout the country.[18] He indicated that lawyers were overrepresented in the legislatures, relative to their number in the population as a whole. An investigation of the Michigan legislature reveals that Hyneman's finding is still applicable to Michigan. Implicit in his finding was the suggestion that lawyers would constitute a conservative bloc in a legislature.[19] A more recent study has disputed this theory.[20] Derge concluded that, as a group, there was no correlation between lawyers and conservatism.[21] Hyneman also noted that the industrial proletariat enjoyed comparatively little membership in the state legislatures.[22] Ostensibly, this is still valid in Michigan where currently, only 8% of the Senate and 6% of the House hold membership in labor unions. However, this factor does not necessarily mean that labor interests are not represented in the Michigan legislature. Organizations such as the UAW and the AFL-CIO are important interest groups in the legislature. This will be explored further in a later chapter.

An examination of Table 2 also demonstrates a variation in the highest level of education attained by the legislators in the years 1962 and 1972. In 1962, 15% of the Senators and 8% of the Representatives had not proceeded beyond elementary school. In the same year, those legislators completing high school only numbered 11 and 49, or 32% and 49% in the Senate and the House respectively. Ten years later, these figures had changed. The Senate in 1972 had 5% of its members with only a grade school education and 39% having completed high school. The Representatives in the House in 1972 had 3% of their number with only an elementary school education, while 45% had completed high school. The trend, then, seems to be toward a more educated legislature. It is interesting that the education level of Michigan's legislators is above the average level in the state. This coincides with a finding by Thomas R. Dye — that in general, state legislators are better educated than those they represent.[23]

TABLE 2

COMPOSITION OF THE MICHIGAN LEGISLATURE[a]

	1972		1962	
	Senate	House	Senate	House
Average Age	48.8	49.7	55.3	53.1
Professional Background	N=31[b]	N=92	N=34	N=110
Attorney	29%	21%	29%	8%
Businessman	16%	17%	24%	23%
Farmer	3%	9%	12%	19%
Real Estate	6%	8%	9%	16%
Teacher	19%	10%	0	2%
Other	29%	2%	18%	18%
Religion	N=33	N=92	N=27	N=96
Protestant	67%	66%	74%	73%
Catholic	27%	33%	18%	25%
Jewish	6%	1%	4%	0
Education	N=38	N=110	N=34	N=110
Grade School Only	5%	3%	15%	8%
High School Only	39%	45%	32%	45%
B.A. or B.S. Only	18%	30%	24%	36%
M.A., J.D., or L.L.B.	37%	22%	29%	11%
Ph.D.	0	1%	0	0
Miscellaneous	N=38	N=110	N=34	N=110
Vetrans	39%	41%	35%	30%
Labor Union Members	8%	6%	6%	8%
Prior Pol. Experience	58%	39%	44%	28%
Negroes	5%	12%	0	8%
Women	0	6%	0	4%

aStatistics are calculated from: State of Michigan, Michigan Manual, Department of Administration, 1961-1962 and 1971-1972.

bN is not constant because in some instances, this information was not available in the Michigan Manual.

The predominant religion in Michigan is Protestant. About two-thirds of all of Michigan's legislators are of this denomination, as of the 1972 legislature. In 1962, the Protestant legislators made up about 73%

of the total. In the 1972 legislature, 27% of the Senators and 33% of the Representatives were Catholic. This figure is slightly above the Catholic population in Michigan as a whole. According to the 1970 census, 26.9% of the state's population is Catholic. The vast majority of Catholic members of the Michigan State Legislature are affiliated with the Democratic party. In the Senate, 1% are Catholic Republicans, while in the House, 13% of the Catholics belong to the Republican party.[24]

In the 1972 legislature, there were two blacks elected to the Senate and thirteen elected to the state House. This was an increase over the number of Negro legislators elected to the legislature in 1962. At that time, there were no black members of the Senate, while there were nine black Representatives elected to the House. All of Michigan's Negro legislators are members of the Democratic party.

The figures for women legislators are similar to those which are applicable to the number of black legislators. In 1972, Michigan had no women Senators and seven female Representatives, or 6% of the House. Ten years previously, the figures were not very different. Again there were no women elected to the Senate and only 4% elected to the House. All of the female legislators in the state are members of the Democratic party. When Dye investigated state legislators, he found that women were greatly under-represented and rarely accounted for more than 5% of the membership of any state legislature.[25]

In 1962, 44% of the Senators and 28% of the Representatives in the House included mention of some prior political experience in their biographies, before being elected to their legislative positions. Ten years later, these figures had increased. In the 1972 legislature, 58% of the Senators and 39% of the Representatives had some previous political experience prior to their current office.

Another fact of some importance is the age of the legislators. In 1962, Senators averaged 55.3 years of age and Representatives averaged 53.1 years. The 1972 legislature was younger in comparison. A member of the state Senate averaged 48.8 years, while the average age of a House member was 49.7 years. The youngest Senator in 1972 was twenty-five years of age, and the oldest member of the Senate was seventy-one that same year. Ten years earlier, the Michigan state Senate consisted of thirty-four members. Under the 1963 Michigan constitution, this number was increased to thirty-eight. At the same time, there were 110 members in the House of Representatives, the same level it presently holds.

Until the mid-1960's, the members of Michigan's legislature were not elected to office according to population, resulting in inequalities within the assembly. According to one political scientist, malapportionment gave the Republican party an advantage in Michigan.[26] Included in this advantage was a benefit to organized agricultural interests regarding this group's influence over state legislation. This did not indicate a necessarily large number of farmers in the legislature; rather, the rural interests were well represented by small town lawyers and businessmen.[27] Malapportionment simultaneously placed labor groups at a comparative disadvantage. However, Baker was careful to indicate that on many issues, rural legislators shared a community of interests with urban legislators who represented a similar social and/or economic perspective.[28]

In 1964, the Michigan legislature experienced a landmark year. The *Reynolds v. Sims* decision went into effect and, for the first time, both houses of the legislature were elected solely on the basis of population.[29] For the first time in approximately thirty years, the Democratic party captured both chambers of the legislature.[30] The Democratic House and Senate majorities were seventy-three to thirty-seven and twenty-three to fifteen respectively. These were the largest majorities the Democrats had ever obtained over the Republicans — before or since that year. Coupled with the reapportionment decision was Barry Goldwater's presidential candidacy in 1964. Lyndon Johnson won the state of Michigan with 66.7% of the popular vote.[31] Obviously, this was a landslide victory and undoubtedly this presidential victory did much to reinforce the Democratic party and help its members gain control of the state legislature. Since that time, the Democrats have been able to maintain a substantial amount of control in the House of Representatives, although the figures do not approach their 1964 majority. The Republicans, however, retained their majority control in the Senate — albeit by a very slender margin — until they lost their majority in the 1974 elections.

Without question, the turning point for the Michigan state legislature was 1964. After that year there was a tangible break with the past. The following is a description of the legislature during the 1930's as viewed by one legislator who served in the House at that time and returned in 1964, where he has continued to serve as a member of that body.

TABLE 3

PARTY DISTRIBUTION IN MICHIGAN'S
FORMER LEGISLATURESa

Year	Senators			Representatives	
	Dem.	Rep.		Dem.	Rep.
1925	. .	32		. .	100
1927	. .	32		2	98
1929	. .	32		2	98
1931	1	31		2	98
1933	17	15		55	45
1935	11	21		49	51
1937	17	15		60	40
1939	9	23		27	73
1941	10	22		32	68
1943	7	25		26	74
1945	8	24		34	66
1947	4	28		5	95
1949	9	23		39	61
1951	7	25		34	66
1953	8	24		34	66
1955b	11	23		51	59
1957	11	23		49	61
1959	12	22		55	55
1961	12	22		54	56
1963	11	23		52	58
1965	23	15		73	37
1967	18	20		54	56
1969	18	20		57	53
1971	19	19		58	52
1973	19	19		60	50
1975	24	14		66	44

a State of Michigan, **Michigan Manual, 1973-1974** Department of Administration, pp. 99-100.

b Reapportionment increased the number of Senators from 32 to 34 and the number of Representatives from 100 to 110 in 1955. Again, in 1965, the number of Senators was increased to 38, under the 1963 constitution.

> All of the space that was allocated to the legislature in those days was the chambers in which the sessions are held and a row of committee rooms in the gallery area for each chamber. It wouldn't exceed more than five or six committee rooms at the most for each body, and in each one of those committee rooms there'd be probably about five different committees. And we had no staff — I mean secretarial staff. And no place to do anything on the floor of the chamber. And no electric voting machine, no loud speakers, no telephones on the floor of the chamber, as they were out in the lobby. There were three or four booths where you could go and place a long distance call at our own expense . . . We were working out at our own desks on the floor [of the House or Senate] which made it very convenient for the lobbyists . . . they could go from desk to desk and help them with their problems. . . .

As late as 1964, no member of the legislature had his own private office. The ratio of secretaries to legislators was one to sixteen. Until the fall of that year, the legislature shared the Capitol Building — an old Victorian structure built sometime during the early 1890's — with the governor and his staff, the state Supreme Court, and various administrative agencies. After the elections, this situation began to change:

> This transition started largely following the November elections in 1964. At that time, Mr. Kowalski, who was Speaker of the House, took things into his own hands somehow and got a lot of agencies evicted and more space utilized, until now there is very little left in the Capitol except the legislators and the Governor's office. And he has, of course, many of his staff at other locations.

This description of the legislature in 1964 by the legislator mentioned previously is corroborated by another member of the legislature, a man who was first elected to the state Senate in 1964:

> When I came here, we had one secretary for sixteen men. Now, here in the Senate and in the House, everybody has their own secretary. And in the Senate we have an aide plus a couple of people on the staff. It's a small staff, but it has improved one hundred percent.

This legislator credited reapportionment with causing the transition which occurred. He continues:

> That was the real breakthrough . . . 1964. It was the first time in thirty years that the Democrats had taken over the legislature. That was the time we began to get staff. In fact, when I came here it had been thirty years under Republicans. One secretary to sixteen men, no offices at all, no phones, no access to books, no access to heads of departments. You operated right from your desk on the floor, with constituents, lobbyists, . . . it was a . mess! So there really has been a tremendous change and the Republicans have followed through.

These changes were visible not only within the legislature but outside of it as well. A survey taken in Michigan noted that after the reapportionment of the legislature, people perceived the legislators of both parties as being of a higher calibre.[32] It was also noted that the Michigan legislators were younger, better educated, and much better paid than their predecessors prior to reapportionment.[33] The heaviest losses in representation resulting from reapportionment were felt by Michigan's rural districts. Although large cities have had some increase in their representation, the most significant gains have been in the suburban districts.[34] In a book published in 1966, Gordon Baker predicted that, on the basis of then-current population trends, future reapportionment would benefit suburban areas.[35] Evidence lends support to that thesis.[36]

The current trend in regard to the legislature appears to favor those members affiliated with the Democratic party.[37] After the elections in November, 1974, the Democrats increased their majority in the House of Representatives to 60% and, for the first time in ten years, they recaptured the majority in the Senate. Since 1966, the Democrats have been increasing their numbers in both the House and the Senate. The 1974 elections gave the Democrats firm control over both chambers of the legislature.

Following the 1970 elections, the state Senate was equally divided between the Democrats and the Republicans — nineteen to nineteen. The Republican party was able to retain its control over the Senate because the Lieutenant Governor was a Republican and it was, and is, his duty to preside over the Senate and to cast his vote in the event of a tie.[38] After the 1970 census, a new redistricting plan, known as the Hatcher-Kleiner Plan, was drawn up and scheduled to go into effect for the House in the 1972 elections and for the Senate in the 1974 fall elections. Under this plan, Detroit's representation in the Senate was reduced from eight-and-one-half to six-and-one-half seats. These two Senate positions have been absorbed by the suburban areas in the counties surrounding Detroit — Oakland, Macomb, and parts of Wayne. During the decade of the 1960's, these counties increased their population, while Detroit's declined. The Republicans had feared that the outcome of the 1974 November elections would reduce their strength. The elections more than fulfilled their worst expectations. The Republican party had estimated that, because of the redistricting plan, the Democrats would secure twenty seats while the Republicans could be assured of only thirteen.[39] It was their belief that only five seats would be contested.[40] In the 1974 elections, the Republicans were elected to only one of the five uncontested seats, giving the Democrats a twenty-four to fourteen majority in the Senate. Thus the Democrats are assured of control in the Senate at least until 1978.

In 1972, after the Hatcher-Kleiner Plan had gone into effect in the House of Representatives, the Democrats had increased their majority in the House from fifty-eight members in 1970 to sixty representatives in 1972. The Republicans in the House dropped from fifty-two to fifty members. Detroit's voice in the House was reduced from twenty-five representatives to twenty, as a result of reapportionment.[41] Based on the 1972 election results, the Democrats appear to have twenty-nine safe — i.e., where a candidate received over 65% of the electoral vote — seats in the House and the Republicans seem to have twenty-four safe seats. If electoral victories of between fifty-five and sixty-five percent are referred to as semi-competitive, then the Democrats have eighteen and the Republicans have twenty of these seats. The Democrats have thirteen competitive seats and the Republicans have six, where competitive indicates a victory of less than fifty-five percent of the electoral vote. Thus, approximately 48% of the seats in the Michigan House of Representatives are considered safe, whereas only 17% of these seats can be regarded as competitive. In all likelihood, the Democrats will continue to maintain a majority — and thus, control the legislature — throughout the decade.

---

[1] Ferris E. Lewis, **State and Local Government in Michigan** (Boston: Allyn and Bacon Inc., 1965), p. 30.

[2] Michigan, **Constitution,** Art. 4, secs. 1-53.

[3] **Ibid.,** Art. 4, sec. 14.

[4] **Ibid.,** Art. 4, sec. 16.

[5] The Council of State Governments, **The Book of the States, 1974-1975** (Lexington, Kentucky, 1974), p. 66.

[6] Michigan, **Constitution,** Art. 4, sec. 7.

[7] State of Michigan, **Michigan Manual,** The Department of Administration, 1973-1974, p. 185.

[8] **Ibid.**

[9] **Ibid.**

[10] **Ibid.**

[11] Michigan, **Constitution,** Art. 4, sec. 3.

[12] The Council of State Governments, **op. cit.,** p. 67.

[13] State of Michigan, **op. cit.,** pp. 199-200.

[14] **Ibid.**

[15] **Ibid.**

[16] State of Michigan, 1971-1972, **op. cit.,** pp. 193-217. This data has been compiled from the biographical sketches of the legislators. Further information may be found in Table 2, on page 29.

[17] **Ibid.**

[18] Charles Hyneman, "Who Makes Our Laws," **Political Science Quarterly,** LV, (1940), p. 558.

[19] **Ibid.,** pp. 556-581.

[20] David R. Derge, "The Lawyer as Decision-Maker in the American State Legislature," **Journal of Politics,** XXI, (August, 1959), p. 427.

[21] **Ibid.**

[22] Hyneman, **op. cit.,** p. 556-581.

[23] Thomas R. Dye, **Politics in States and Communities** (Englewood Cliffs, New Jersey: Prentice-Hall, Inc., 1973), p. 124.

[24] State of Michigan, 1971-1972, **op. cit.,** pp. 193-217.

[25] Dye, **op. cit.,** p. 124.

[26] Gordon E. Baker, **Rural v. Urban Political Power** (Garden City, N.Y.: Doubleday and Co., Inc. 1955), p. 20.

[27] **Ibid.,** p. 24.

[28] **Ibid.**

[29] **Reynolds** v. **Sims,** 84 S.Ct. 1362 (1964).

[30] State of Michigan, 1973-1974, **op. cit.,** pp. 99-100. For further information, please refer to **Table 3,** p. 32.

[31] State of Michigan, 1971-1972, **op. cit.,** p. 119.

[32] Carolyn Steiber, **The Politics of Change in Michigan** (Lansing, Mich.: Michigan State University Press, 1970), p. 86.

[33] **Ibid.**

[34] William J. Keefe and Morris S. Ogul, **The American Legislative Process: Congress and the States** (Englewood Cliffs, N.J.: Prentice-Hall Inc., 1968), p. 93.

[35] Gordon E. Baker, **The Reapportionment Revolution** (New York: Random House, 1966), p. 60.

[36] Keefe and Ogul, **op. cit.,** p. 93.

[37] In the 1974 elections, the Democrats of both houses won with larger majorities than their Republican counterparts.

[38] State of Michigan, 1973-1974, **op. cit.,** p. 49.

[39] **The Detroit Free Press,** November 9, 1972, p. 14A.

[40] **Ibid.**

[41] **The Detroit News,** May 5, 1972, p. 3A.

CHAPTER IV

THE LEGISLATORS

If governments are to be supplied with high talents, political recruitment should have a high priority on the party agenda. The recruiters must know how to select from the possible candidates, those most likely to contribute action and rationality to the governmental process, to attract them to governmental careers, and to retain them in office once elected. In this task must depends, it appears, on personal motivation for office-seeking and on satisfactions that individuals derive from holding office.[1]

What are some of the factors that influence an individual in such a way that he will direct his career toward politics, specifically to the state legislature? Political socialization appears to commence, most frequently, in early childhood.[2] This fact was corroborated in the personal interviews which were conducted for this dissertation. Most legislators who were interviewed indicated that their interest in politics first surfaced during their childhood, or at least in some phase of their adolescence.[3] When asked at what point in their lives their interest in politics first began, many legislators responded as in this excerpt from one of the interviews: "I can't recall when I wasn't interested in politics. When I was six or seven years old, I can recall in my neighborhood being very pro-Roosevelt man when Landon was running for President [sic].

Another legislator, who is quoted in the segment that follows, was not only socialized very early but, in addition, his father was a state Representative. When questioned about his early interest in politics, he replied:

It's kind of hereditary, as when I was just a few years old my father was in the House of Representatives four years. And then he was a delegate to the constitutional convention in 1908 . . . In those days he'd bring the delegates home for the weekend at the farm and they'd talk, talk, talk. And I'd listen. And then I came down here. [Lansing] and visited the constitutional convention with him a few times. Well then, in 1913 and '14, '15, and '16 he was a member of the state Senate and I was the youngest child. And rather than leave me home, me and my mother came down here and roomed down here. So I was fitted out with a job as a page in the state Senate and served in that capacity whenever the legislature was in session during those four years.

Another important factor that proved instrumental in directing an individual's attention in the direction of a career in politics was participation by that individual in a political campaign, to some degree.[4] One legislator described his participation in the Presidential campaign in 1924. He was just twelve years of age at the time, and was a dedicated boy scout. His primary function in the political campaign involved the distribution of red, white and blue stickers that encouraged the people to vote. He went from house to house in his home district of Benton Harbor, passing out these stickers. This was a sufficient stimulus to affect his selection of a career later on in his life — this one simple experience.

Other legislators attributed their career selection to a particular event or condition. Two legislators who were interviewed for this study stated that specific situations were responsible, to a very large degree, for their decision to make politics their careers. One of these legislators, a woman who has served in the Michigan House of Representatives for many years, claimed her entrance into politics was a matter of self defense.

> I came to a new community when I was first married . . . it was just beginning to build up. Ford Motors had moved in from Highland Park and we bought a new home. We were interested in seeing good houses in the neighborhood, and the first thing that happened was, they put up a tarpaper shack for a hamburger stand. This aroused the people, so then we got busy on zoning, and we rezoned . . . People got acquainted with me. So then we set up a building code for our city and people began to say they'd like me to run for council. And I said "no, I wasn't interested in politics." . . . People insisted, and I was elected to the council.

For this Representative, this experience was the first step to what has proven to be a lengthy career in politics.

The interviews which were conducted for this paper have illustrated the early politicalization of Michigan's legislators. This coincides with an earlier study by Heinz Eulau.[5] The results of Eulau's study indicate that about one-third of the state legislators surveyed recalled their childhood, or grammar school period, as the time they first became aware of politics.[6] Approximately one-half of the legislators had developed their political awareness in the years following elementary school but preceding college.[7] Yet a sizeable number did not become interested in politics until their adult years.[8] The study further established that, in general, legislators tend to come from families who are involved in politics to a greater extent than the average family.[9] Another, more recent, study indicated that child rearing practices may be the most significant factor which affects personality in politically relevant ways.[10] This reinforces the theory that it is the family that plays the most important role in awakening an interest in politics.[11] Eulau found that the study of civics, politics, or related subjects in an academic environment did not stimulate political interest.[12] He also noted that such an important occurrence as a war, an economic depression, or a Presidential election may provoke political interest.[13]

Interest alone is not usually sufficient to launch an individual on a career in politics. Three other factors which are closely related to a candidate's willingness to seek elective office are: motivation, resources, opportunity.[14] One important motivating factor that was expressed frequently by the legislators interviews and throughout the questionnaires was the opportunity to effect change. Here are some common responses to the question of motivation:

> I basically enjoy the new politics kind of thing where the people are concerned about government as a tool for helping people.

> I think I've been interested in reform. Basically, I'm steeped in reform and therefore I look around the various occupations, various roles that one can play. And I find government offers the nearest thing to some kind of effective concern and where I can apply the talent that I've used.

> I think politics is one of the vehicles to bring about change in society. And I think that society is dynamic and there are needs for change. There are some immoralities existing in society that need changing — the racial issue, the question of poverty. I think that whether one likes politics or not, most of the decisions that bring about a profound change in society have some political ramifications to them.

Still other legislators found that the concept of public service was, to them, a motivating force. For example:

> I think politics . . . is service to people. Very little of it is really partisan politics. Ninety-five percent of the bills that go through this legislature having nothing to do, really, with the Democratic or Republican party. They're supported from a bipartisan standpoint. So a great deal of my work really lies in my service to the constituency. Getting their problems resolved, cutting through the red tape of the bureaucracy, getting answers for them — quite a lot of our time is spent in this way.

Yet another reason for entering politics as a career is the excitement that is engendered by being at the core of the important foci of power. Relative to this factor is the thrill of the game. As one legislator put it:

> I just thought it would be an exciting departure. I'm a lawyer. It's where the action is. It's an opportunity to do something rather than talk about it.

In a similar vein, another legislator gave this response:

> I guess as a worker the excitement, the opportunity of meeting candidates, working with them, seeing them going down and knowing that they were writing laws that were important. I have a great love of government. I think it's an exciting area and now that I'm into it, I think that for somebody who wants to shape things or do things as a career, it has more potential than any other career.

A recent investigation by John Parker established four classifications of the motivating forces which induce candidates to initially run for office.[15] The first category is the Material factor.[16] This encompasses those qualities which contribute to the betterment of an individual's position. It involves a desire to step up from a previous job. The salary may provide an inducement. Another aspect is the perception of political activity as beneficial to one's own business. Finally, seeking political office may enable an individual to escape from a routine or boring job. It is interesting to note that none of the legislators interviewed for this dissertation made mention of the qualities ascribed to the Material factor. It is likely that, because the legislators perceive themselves as selfless public servants, the motive of bettering their own personal positions would not be consciously acknowledged.

Parker's second classification is the Solidary factor.[17] This involves a desire to attain a position of leadership, a fascination with politics, a desire to be among important people, and a need to be recognized in the community. The Purposive factor is the third classification.[18] This applies to those individuals who are motivated by a desire to promote specific policies, who possess some degree of disatisfaction with the incumbent office holder, and who want to be involved in public service. The final classification is the Asked To Run factor, where an individual has been requested to seek office by public officials, party officials, friends, or relatives.[19] According to Parker's study, these are the four most significant motivating factors in inducing an individual to seek election to his first political office.

Following motivation, the second vital factor which assists in a candidate's determination to seek political office is his accessibility to resources — both financial and human. A potential candidate must honestly question whether or not he possesses the necessary skills, the money, or access to funding, and the time required to launch and carry out a credible campaign. Most of the legislators who participated in the discussions admitted that, in their first campaign, their organization was extremely simple. One Senator explained that his entire organization consisted solely of his wife and himself.

In his recently published study of recruitment practices in Oregon, Lester Seligman noted the importance of family and friends in a candidate's initial decision to seek elective office.[20] When the candidacy was opposed by family and friends, the individual would decline to run, even if the success of the campaign seemed assured.[21] Seligman also observed that, as a campaign progresses, the original circle of family, friends, and others who supported the candidate from the inception of his campaign would enlarge and develop into a full-fledged campaign organization.[22] As the campaign continues, additional backers or new sponsors will come forward and offer their support.

The majority of campaign funds is expended on materials, advertising, and, when the finances are sufficient, a campaign headquarters. The possession of campaign headquarters is significant because of its inherent ability to attract volunteer help and to familiarize the local neighborhood with the name, and often the image, of the candidate. What follows are descriptions of three different campaigns by various legislators. The first two examples are from campaigns conducted in rural areas, while the third is a descriptive account of a campaign in a densely populated metropolitan area.

I've always had to finance quite a share of each campaign out of my own pocket. And what I would get in contributions wasn't anywhere near compared with what I put out in newspaper and radio advertising. I don't have any billboards or any television exposure. I do very little advertising in each paper in the district and each radio station in the district. We go around in a bunch of cars, and then we have a loud-speaker along, maybe a little kid band or something to make a little confusion.

I just had fantastic volunteer help, mostly from kids. There were a couple of women who gave me all their kids and their kids' friends ... I still remember. I started on May 7, 1968, in the city of Langsberg in southwestern Shiawassee County going around knocking door-to-door. And that was just about three months before the primary, which was on August 6th that year. And by the time the Saturday previous to the primary rolled around, and that was August 3rd, I covered, or my wife covered, or one of my volunteers covered every single house and dwelling in the entire 87,000 district. Now that — and I don't mean just ... villages or cities. I mean we went up and down country roads and ran up lawns and knocked on porch doors. Sometimes the farmer wasn't home and we stuck something in the door. In other words, we may not have had contact with everybody in the house, but we left something. And then, in addition to that, I went to all these 'Meet the Candidate' meetings. I set up meetings myself. I asked to go appear before groups. I wrote my own press releases on what I said, afterwards, and gave it to the newspapers. And I hit shopping centers. It was getting to the point where, by the end of the campaign, I mean, I was hitting people for the third and fourth and fifth time. And people were just saying ... 'you again, you're just everywhere. You're big with us, you know.' And the organization was that way... In that district, again, it's not a concentrated district ... I mean, this was a district that covered all of Shiawassee County which, by itself ... it would be like covering, physically, the area of Oakland County and one-third of Macomb. But of course, there were only 80,000 people in it. But the more spread out it is, the more difficult it is. And we covered it. And I did everything. And I had radio advertising, I had billboards, I had newspaper advertising, I had matches. I had a really beautiful campaign brochure that we put together, and then I had campaign cards on top of that. Actually, I was not the biggest spender in that race ... I spent about $10,000 and I was second in spending... But I spent enough to get the message across, to get my name around. But at the same time, I think it was the personal contact and the unrelenting effort, door-to-door campaigning that did it and it paid off.

Campaigns cost money. Therefore you've got to go out and raise the money. And that means fund-raisers, that means, usually, a cocktail party and a series of things like that. And those always concern you because there's always a possibility you're going to bomb out and not do too well. And also . . . a fund raiser probably requires a higher degree of organization than anything else you do in the campaign, because it really doesn't matter whether you campaign in this street or over in another neighborhood, as long as you're campaigning. But you have to be very careful in having a fund raiser — be sure all of the follow-up work is done and so on . . . My basement has been the scene of many, many campaign meetings, all of which I have enjoyed.

The third contributing factor which assists a potential candidate in his decision to seek office is opportunity. Such an individual may possess the interest and the resources, but unless be believes he has a chance to win in his election bid, it is unlikely he will enter the contest. As some of the legislators indicated in their interviews and question-naires, unless they felt they could win their election, they decided not to run. Three examples taken from the interviews will further illustrate this point:

I took a look at the district I ran in, to assess my possibilities. I took into account the fact that I had been in that area for twenty years, and I felt that the possibility of my being elected was better than anyone else had in the area. The fact that I wasn't running against an incumbent . . .

Well, I think partly the fact that the incumbent had retired, that it was a district that I could get elected in . . . I'm sure that if the incumbent hadn't retired — he'd been in twenty-eight years — that I wouldn't have run.

It was an area where I was well known. I taught school there in Flint for eight years and I knew a lot of people. The district actually encompassed pretty well the high school district where I had taught, so I was well known. That was certainly a factor. One doesn't run unless he feels there's a reasonable chance of winning.

Seligman's study of recruitment noted that candidates fall into four categories.[23] First, there are the agents — those who represent interest groups.[24] The second group consists of those individuals who consent to run for office because of party loyalty; these are the con-scripted candidates.[25] The co-opted candidates comprise the third category.[26] These are prominent individuals, such as civic leaders, members of the news media, famous atheletes, members of old families, etc., who are persuaded to run in order to strengthen the party ticket. Finally, there are the self-starters — candidates who run without apparent sponsors.[27]

The vast majority of the Michigan legislators who were interviewed perceived themselves as self-starters — at least in their initial candidacy. This may be explained by the fact that all the interviews were conducted with office holders. That is to say, those candidates who where unsuccessful in their quest for office were not included in the interviews. Thus, many individuals who became candidates reluctantly were not accounted for. It is this last group that usually falls into the conscripted candidate category, for it is in futile contests that the party must frequently recruit candidates.[28] Another factor which helps to explain the large number of self-starters in the legislature is Michigan's use of direct primaries. Seligman has stated that "the direct primary is favorable for self-starters because party organizations cannot block self-promotion."[29]

V.O. Key once stated that perhaps one of the most important functions party leaders have to perform is the recruitment of candidates for office.[30] And indeed, a few legislators who were interviewed acknowledged that they had been approached by party leaders and encouraged to campaign.[31] One Representative recounted his experience thusly:

> Actually, some friends approached me late in 1961. I was approached by them — a state Representative and his son, both very good friends of mine — and they said "Why don't you run for city council?" My immediate response was "Hell my wife won't vote for me if I run; who's going to vote for me? I don't know how to campaign." They said: "Well, we do. We'll help you." So I ran . . .

However, Key was aware that the party generally is negligent in this aspect of its function.[32] Once the candidates make their decision to seek elective office, the majority of these individuals received little, if any, assistance from their political parties — neither in the primary elections nor in the general election.[33] One legislator, a member of the Democratic party who ran as a party member in his bid for office, discussed what he perceived to be a lack of party organization at the local level:

> The Democratic party is really quite disorganized on a local level. Under Neil Staebler, it was organized on a state level and that's pretty well gone now. But I know on a county level that if no Democrat filed for state Representative . . . that the party wouldn't know about it until the day after. The Democratic party, on a local level, is almost non-existent. The Democratic party comes into being every two years. There's no permanent headquarters. There is a chairman. We don't have meetings that often. If I depended upon the Democratic party to get me elected — forget it. Really! . . . I went to the first meeting of the county committee to, hopefully, get some dollars for my campaign and they assessed me one hundred dollars, which I never paid. So it's usually broke. The party is usually broke at the local level.

The Republican party organization does not appear to be very different from its Democratic party counterpart. One Republican legislator indicated that it was not the party's policy to take an active role in recruiting nor to involve itself in primary races. To a large extent, whether or not a candidate is able to obtain assistance from his respective political party is determined by a multitude of factors. The financial status of the party at the local level is one element which is taken into consideration by the party. Another important factor is whether or not the candidate is an incumbent. Relative to this last point is the question of the candidate's chance to win. If the race seems difficult for the candidate, the party may be reluctant to make any contribution to what they may regard as a lost cause. Yet another element in the determination of party involvement in a candidate's campaign is his standing within the party. An individual who has been active and worked in co-operation with his party is more likely to receive party assistance than is a candidate who has defied party policy and pursued his own individual course of action.

The role which the parties play varies from county to county. What now follows is a description by one Representative of his personal efforts to improve the organization of his party at the county level. In his case, the county — Oakland County — includes many of the suburbs north of the city of Detroit.[34]

> Our county party in Oakland County has grown tremendously in the last six or seven years. When I came, I was Deputy Chairman. In '65 we were broke. We had very little in the way of resources. One of the first things I did was put all of Oakland County's registered voters on computer tape . . . We began a strong identification program, identifying who are the Democratic families, who are the Republican families. We now have that coded on our computer tapes. Now the party is in a position to offer the candidate something meaningful — mailing labels of registered voters, mailing labels of Democratic families. Now, that is political muscle. We've got something like that, and so the party increasingly is having effect in individual campaigns. This year for example, 1972, the County Committee felt that it was strong enough, both organizationally and financially, in terms of vote-getting potential to endorse candidates in primaries. They only endorsed candidates seeking countywide offices — prosecutors, the sheriff, etc. . . Also, the party, I think, this year as in the past, will have a number of campaign offices . . . It will be staffed by a full-time person whose job it will be to bring in volunteers to help myself and other candidates. . . They contribute volunteers to do distribution, for example, that will benefit all of the candidates, or they'll be canvassing for identification. Well, the end result of that is to help me to pull Democrats out to vote on election day, and that's very helpful to me.

Even on the rare occasion when the party was well-organized, all the Representatives who were interviewed stated that they relied primarily on their own personal staffs and on their own ability to raise money for their respective campaigns. The organization of the legislators is largely an independent and personal one. Thus, when they are elected to office they are independent of their political party to a very great extent. Consequently, the legislators do not feel compelled to vote according to the party's line.[35] Party discipline is difficult to maintain.[36] It is very rare for either party to attempt to discipline one of its members. If a party member has consistently taken anti-party positions and if the party believes there is a chance to successfully punish that individual, it may decide to take some action. The most drastic form of discipline is the purge — that is, to defeat the individual in an election. Since the legislator has his own organization for the most part and little, if any, contact with the party organization, purging is a very difficult form of discipline to accomplish. However, there have been a few successful attempts.

One such case was that of Richard Friske, Republican from the 106th District, elected to the House of Representatives in 1970. In 1972, the Republican party decided to purge Friske from the legislature. This case was unique for several reasons. Friske was born in Poland and flew in the German air force during the Second World War. After the War, he emigrated to this country and settled in Michigan. Soon after his arrival he joined the John Birch Society. In 1970, he was elected to the state House as the Representative from Charlevoix. In discussing this event, one legislator recalled that Friske had been elected on a fluke. His particular district represented about eight different counties and, at the time, eleven candidates were seeking the office. While Friske had an entrenched bloc of right-wing support, the remaining candidates eliminated one another. As a Republican candidate in a Republican district, Friske was elected to the House in the general election. In 1972 there was a determined effort by the Republican organization to defeat Friske and remove him from the Michigan political scene. Governor Milliken endorsed another Republican candidate running against Friske in the primary, as did the Michigan Education Association, an influential lobby in the state. According to another interviewee, it seemed that everybody was "out to get" Friske — and they did. However, this drastic form of discipline is very rare. More often than not, a legislator will be admonished by the party officials if he repeatedly ignores party policy. That is about the extent to which the party hierarchy generally goes. Again, the organization of the parties varies from city to city and from district to district, being somewhat more effective at the local or county level than at the state level. This is the case in most states, and is not confined to Michigan.[37]

The cost of campaigning varies from election to election and is dependent, to a large extent, on the strength of the opposition. The cost of running a campaign for the office of state Senator would be approximately nine thousand dollars, while a typical campaign for election to the House of Representatives in Michigan would cost about

$6,500.[38] These costs can vary a great deal, depending on resources and circumstances, among other factors. One legislator whom I interviewed spent only five hundred dollars on his campaign, while another spent as much as twenty thousand dollars on a very difficult campaign. As one legislator put it:

> Well, it depends, of course, on the campaign. My primary expenses this year 1972 is going to be very minimal, because I have no opposition...But when I first ran, I had very strong and effective opposition in the primary in 1970... I raised and spent six thousand dollars just in my primary. And then, in the general, turned around and spent another six thousand dollars ... It was just one of those things. The tougher it is the harder you have to work, the more money you have to spend. You take out those newspaper ads, you do those things because you have to, because your opponent is doing it.

The same Representative went on to describe the advantages of an incumbent in waging a campaign for re-election.

> An incumbent has a number of built-in advantages. First and foremost, he has been servicing the district for, in my case, almost two years. He's been making speeches around the district. I doubt if there is a service club in ... that I haven't spoken before at least once. And I always tell them "Ask me back; I'll come back." So you have that kind of an advantage. You have a built-in core of volunteers. You have your people who have contributed to fund-raisers in the past and, unless you've been a very bad legislator and turned them off, you know they're going to help you again. In addition, the office itself has a built-in advantage. We do have mailing privileges. My mailing privileges are sufficient, even as a freshman, and the longer you're there, the better your mailing privileges get. Even as a freshman I have the ability to mail every resident in my district every three or four months. That means I can get three or four mailings a year into every home in my district. Well, that's just a fantastic advantage. It's not the kind of literature that says vote for me, but what it can say is, how do you feel about issues A, B, C, and D. It can say, here is what I have done about issues A, B, C, and D as your Representative. Of course, every time you send that newsletter out it's got your picture or it's got your name on it and it doesn't have to say vote for me. All it has to do is say, "I'm your Representative and here's what I'm doing." And you get that into people's homes over a period of two years. And then an opponent runs against you and maybe, with his best resources, maybe he can afford one mailing throughout the district and one door-to-door distribution. Well, you're going to do that too. Plus you've got all this other stuff, all this backlog of mail. So I think you'd be able to maintain a generally favorable image.

Once the candidates are elected, they must then take on and face up to their responsibilities as legislators. The manner in which they meet these responsibilities depends, to a certain degree, on what they perceive to be essential to constitute an effective legislator. Not surprisingly, a plurality of those interviewed thought that the passage of legislation was their most important responsibility. In order to be effective, most thought it was necessary to develop their expertise in the various areas with which they are concerned. To quote one of the legislators who was interviewed:

> I think acquiring knowledge is the big thing, to become knowledgeable as one can be in every area, particularly those areas where he has a higher degree of responsibility . . . Knowledge is power, and one should vote from knowledge and not from ignorance.

However, there was a variety of criteria mentioned that the legislators believed they ought to utilize in order to fulfill their legislative obligations. The passage of sound legislation and the prevention of poor legislation were most frequently mentioned. One legislator defined an effective legislator as "one who is able to inspire confidence in government." Other members of the Michigan assembly emphasized constituent relations as vital to their effectiveness. They felt it was an essential aspect of their position to maintain contact with their constituents, search out the voters' views on the various issues, educate their constituency, and assist their constituents with any problems they might have with the government. A few of the legislators indicated that responding to the needs of the state, rather than limiting themselves to their own local constituents, was of great importance; however, that view was rare. Essentially, the legislators focused their efforts on the passage of good legislation and on meeting the needs of their constituents.

According to many of the legislators, one of the major difficulties with which they have to deal is the organization of their time, so that they are able to get a maximum amount of their work accomplished. For several legislators, there are not enough hours in the day to meet all of their responsibilities. Most Senators and Representatives interviewed reported putting in a minimum of ten hours daily in their offices, and several stated that fifteen hours a day was their norm. One Senator described a typical routine day in the following manner:

> I'd say generally, if we're in a regular routine, about three-and-one-half hours are spent in session. During that same day, we might have two or three hours in committee meetings. The committee meeting is generally in the morning. How, you may spend your noon hour with either one or two lobbyists, or one or two legislators may be involved, and lunch, in that case, would be an hour to an hour-and-a-half, an hour-and-forty-five minutes. Usually our breakfasts are an hour and usually we meet either with constituents or with legislative committee members — something relating to the legislature — or a group from home that just wants to be able to spend a little time with you and talk to you. But that would be your breakfast. You spend about an hour here before you go to a committee meeting. The committee meeting is early. You work that in and then spend an hour or more before lunch here in the office. Right after the session you again meet lobbyists or fellow legislators, or someone else that is waiting for you . . . Generally, I stay in the office until dinner time, and dinners, again, one spends with either clubs or associations.

47

Another Senator indicated the importance that the time of the year plays in determining the number of hours spent on the floor of the legislative chambers:

> Now the floor time depends on the time of the year. Later on in the year, when we get pretty heavy, we'll start sessions at 9:00 or 10:00 A.M. in the morning [sic] and I work here until 4:00 A.M. the following morning; it depends. Early in the year, we're just getting under way. We might spend fifteen to twenty minutes on the floor . . . It's like a freight train taking off — it gains momentum as it goes along . . . If someone came in and took a look at the legislature the first couple of days of the session, he might say: "those fellows don't do anything at all." If he came in and looked at the session in the middle of June, he'd say: "I wouldn't take that job for anything."

The legislators spend their time in a variety of activities, both in their offices and in a combined social/business setting. Among those legislators who were interviewed or responded to the questionnaire, the majority stated that constituent relations occupied more of their time than any other single duty. The following table illustrates the breakdown:

TABLE 4

DISTRIBUTION OF
A LEGISLATOR'S TIME

Activity	Hours/Day
constituent relations	2.8
floor time	2.7
committee sessions	2.4
reading, reviewing legislation	2.2
interest groups	1.0
office management, staff	0.7
total hours spent at the legislature	11.8

*N varies from 21 to a maximum of 31 responses per item contained in this table.

Constituent relations includes, according to the legislators, talking over various issues and assisting with any bureaucratic problems the constituents might bring to their desks, either in-person, by a direct telephone conversation, or through a personal letter to the legislator. Time spent on the floor of both the Senate and the House of Representatives occupied the second largest portion of a legislator's day. This would include the introduction or discussion of legislation. Committee sessions take up approximately 2.4 hours of every legislative day. Since the legislators are members of several different committees, this time is usually divided among these various committees. Reading and reviewing legislation took up a substantial portion of every legislator's day. Studying legislation was essential so that the legislators knew what the various bills which were discussed on the floor and in committee concerned. This activity also assisted them in formulating the questionnaires which the vast majority of legislators send to their constituents on a fairly regular basis. The smallest portion of the legislators' time was spent meeting with interest groups and in the management of their offices and their staffs. Although it was not mentioned in *Table 4,* many of the legislators spend a few hours commuting to and from work each day. Not all of the legislators reside in or very near the state capitol in Lansing; many commute daily from their homes in other areas, such as Detroit or Flint, for example. Meal time was not accounted for in the table either. Most of the legislators combine their lunches, and often their dinners as well, with colleagues or lobbyists in order to discuss business. According to the data received, the average legislator spends close to twelve hours daily at his job. Many also utilize their weekends for additional time. Often this is the time they are able to meet and talk with their constituents — either in Lansing or when they return to their home districts. Based on the information found in *Table 4* and on other data taken from discussions with the legislators, it can be conservatively estimated that the average Michigan state legislator spends about sixty hours every week at his chosen occupation. Even when the state legislature is not in session, many of these legislative functions continue, particularly the relations between the legislators and their constituents. The committees also continue to meet during this time.

In order to assist the newly elected legislators in adapting to their new environment, an orientation program is provided. This program accelerates the period of adjustment that accompanies their new job. Basically, the program informs the new lawmakers as to what services are available to them, in order to assist them in the performance of their legislative duties. What follows is the description of this program, according to one of the legislators:

> I was elected in 1970 — of course, in November. In December they held a . . . workshop for new legislators. And they had some of the older, more experienced guys there to talk to us . . . is in charge of the physical plant. He's

the guy that assigns you an office. He's the guy that sees that you get a secretary . . . any equipment you need — desks, chairs, etc. He gives you the prison industry's catalogue and allows you to select from within that catalogue . . . get up and tells you this is what's available. If you have any problems, see me.If you want dictating equipment, see me. They describe for you, if you want a bill drafted [sic]. Here's the guy you talk to; he's the head of the Service Bureau. He'll assign somebody to draft your bill, and all you have to do is give him one, or two, or three sentence descriptions of what you want and they'll take it from there. They describe your mailing privileges — five thousand dollars a month for freshmen and a ten percent increase annually for every year of service . . . They describe the retirement program that is available to legislators. You get ten percent of your pay and the state contributes so much, and you're eligible after so many years . . . You're told about the various committees and what they do, how they work. It's an orientation in a true sense.

When a legislator first enters the legislature, he is associated with one or the other of the major political parties in Michigan. However, because most of these men are in the legislature as a result of the efforts of their own personal organizations, rather than those of the party, party discipline, as an outside constraint, is weak. It is the legislators' own perceptions of the Democratic and Republican parties that will determine their loyalty and dedication to their respective parties. The following excerpts are taken from various interviews and illustrate the characteristics that these Democratic party members ascribe to both their own party and to the opposition party as well:

Basically, the Republican party is a more business-oriented party. Certainly the distinctions aren't as great as they used to be. The Democrats are business-oriented. One-half of my Senatorial district are business-oriented communities, so I certainly am responsive to them. But overall, you still really think about working people — problems they have. That is, theoretically, the basic thing . . . to try and help the little guy get along and not be squashed. And I think all the progressive legislation — and I mean really progressive legislation, not just superficial — social security, health care — it's all been procreated, generated by the Democratic party . . . I hate to think where we would be if the policies that they opposed never even breathed life. It would be a sad situation.

Basically, the philosophy of the Republican party is that you live within your means, they say, to meet the needs, basically, of their party or different areas than the Democratic party. The Democratic party is more willing to take a chance, more willing to spend a few dollars on credit. They're more willing to go out and embark on new programs, particularly among the poor and in the field of education, because most of us in the Democratic party never had a chance to go to college.

I think the Democratic party, generally speaking, is more willing to question the status quo and use to power of government to change the status quo. I think the Republican party is less willing, or less frequent, in its question of the status quo, is a little more satisfied with the satus quo and is reluctant to use the power of government . . . on the basic nitty-gritty labor issues. You generally find the Democratic party is much more willing to, say, increase workmen's compensation, unemployment compensation, minimum wage, mailing of the unemployment check — elimination of the week's waiting period of unemployment compensation. You'll find the majority of Republicans against it. So on labor issues you can really find the split down here.

It's so clear to me . . . I'm amazed at how the Republicans can vote almost 93% together without a caucus position. There are no minorities — there are no blacks, no women at all in the Republican party. It's interesting. And the Democratic party speaks for itself. It's all over the place. There are Democrats who vote with Republicans, Democrats on what we call the extreme conservative end of the political spectrum. There are some on the extreme right and left. There are women. There are blacks. There are minorities. You name it; it's there. Whereas, the Republican party is almost one hundred percent of one cause, one ethnic affiliation. And they can oft time vote 99% without the help of a caucus . . . The Democratic party needs caucus after caucus because we're all over the place.

Thus, it can be noted that the Democrats perceive themselves as representing the common man — more willing to use the power of government, more inclined to sponsor innovative legislation and to support progressive legislation, more willing to bring about reform. They attribute, to the members of their party, a strong support of the working man. They are inclined to push for programs that are beneficial to labor. They are willing to support deficit finance when they perceive a need for such action. The Democrats also view themselves as more representative of the various minority groups — ethnic, racial, and religious — than their opposition. They see the Republican party as representing the interests of big business, as standing for a balanced budget, possessing a distrust of government, inclined to favor the maintainence of the status quo, and, in general, representative of white, anglo-saxon, protestant America.

Michigan's Republican legislators also have views as to what the Republican and Democratic parties stand for. It can be observed in the excerpts which follow, whether or not there are any significant differences in the perceptions of the parties from the Republican legislators.

I think the Democrats tend toward more state and federal control, versus local government. And I think the Democrats say "Here is a solution; we'll worry about how we are going to pay for it later." The Republicans say "Now wait a minute. That may be a solution but how are we going to pay for it? And we better find a way first." I think fiscal responsibilities and state and federal control versus local control, are the two major differences between the parties, as I've experienced them.

The Democrats have been the voice of organized labor.

Well, I think the Republican party over here is more fiscally responsible . . . Republicans are spread all over the state of Michigan, which is not always the case with the Democratic party. The majority of the people in the Democratic party are coming out of areas like Detroit, Wayne County, Oakland County. So we divide on party lines a lot of times . . . Our party, the geography of the party, makes us a little more diversified and we get involved that way.

It depends very much on what you're talking about. If you're talking about economic issues, I think you could see a difference between Republicans and Democrats here that is fairly profound and fairly certain . . . Most Republicans will tend to be more conservative economically than Democrats on economic issues, but if you talk about social issues, boy, you've got to be careful about making generalizations because you take things like abortion laws — who supported abortion reform in the Michigan legislature? Republicans.

I would think, basically, the main difference is approach to a problem. I would like to think the Republican party tries to look more at the overall picture of the state in dealing with the welfare of the state. Certainly, we believe that the way to deal with the welfare of the state is by job creativity and job placement, rather than by, let's say, penalties against industry or against people with financial means rather that to say it's our responsibility to automatically provide for the poor. Both parties agree that you provide for the poor and the unfortunate. I would like to think that Republicans make that provision by job opportunity and by training, rather than by direct grant to this type of individual. And we think it's dehumanizing to say to a person: "Look, we don't have a job for you. We would rather just give you money and sit back." We think that's dehumanizing.

The Republicans, then, perceive the Democrats as being irresponsible when it comes to spending the state's monies. They perceive their Democratic counterparts as being labor-dominated and being more willing to place people on the welfare roles. Further, they view the Democrats as stressing a more centralized government. Their fellow Republicans, on the other hand, are perceived as being more fiscally responsible, as stressing decentralization and supporting more local control of government, as being economically conservative but socially progressive. The Republicans defend big business because it means more jobs. They perceive themselves as representing a larger geographical area than the Democrats, and in that sense, are more diverse than the Democrats.

These somewhat different perspectives of and by the legislative members of the Democratic and Republican parties are not mutually exclusive. Both agree that the Democrats are more willing to spend state finances on various government programs, that they are more willing to use the power of government for the purpose of reform, and that the Democratic party in Michigan represents the interests of organized labor. Both parties' members in the legislature are in agreement that the Republican legislators are more cautious when it comes to spending for social programs, that they emphasize local control of government agencies, and strongly support a balanced budget and, in general, the maintainence of the status quo. It is also agreed that Republicans are more representative of business interests. The difference in perspectives concerns the degree of progressive, as opposed to conservative, inclinations of the Republican legislators toward social reforms, such as no-fault automobile insurance, the establishment of a state lottery, and abortion reform. Both parties, it would seem, wish to appear as the motivating force behind these changes in Michigan's government.

Much of the preceding discourse, pertaining to political parties in the Michigan state legislature, conforms to other studies which have been conducted on the American party system in general. For example, Frank Sorauf has stated that "all legislative parties are anomalies in their party systems. They share the party's label, its traditions, and at least nominally, its leadership and its fortunes."[39] Sorauf also noted that a legislative party is:

> the product of a conglomeration of local constituencies, and it distrusts attempts to define national party policies and goals . . . In Congress and most state legislatures the legislative party has little disciplinary power over the rank and file of the party membership, and party conferences and caucuses rarely attempt to bind their members.[40]

However, political parties in the Michigan state legislature do serve a legitimate function in the state's political system. There are factors that work to promote party unity and which encourage party responsibility. The governor, if he is a strong executive, is able to utilize pressure, patronage, and his personal leadership to rally his party.[41] The leaders in both legislative chambers may persuade their parties' members to unite on crucial issues. When they were interviewed, the majority of Michigan legislators indicated that they did not adhere to party policy on most legislation. However, in his investigation of state legislatures, Thomas Dye utilized the index of cohesion and determined that, on issues such as taxation, appropriations, welfare, and the regulation of business and labor, the Michigan legislators displayed the greatest party unity.[42] Dye found the mean indix of cohesion in the Michigan legislature to be 81% for the Democrats and 75% for the Republicans.[43] Political parties in Michigan represent separate and distinct socio-economic coalitions. Consequently, party cohesion is particularly evident where economic issues are concerned.[44] Other factors which encourage party unity include the occupational, ethnic, and religious differences between the Democratic and Republican parties, as well as the variant constituencies which each party represents. Furthermore, the legislator's own perception of his party's stand on the issues will affect the degree to which he adheres to the party's line.

---

[1] James D. Barber, **The Lawmakers: Recruitment and Adaptation to Legislative Life.** (New Haven, Conn.: Yale University Press, 1965), p. 9.

[2] John C. Wahlke **et al., The Legislative System** (New York: John Wiley and Sons, Inc., 1962), p. 76.

[3] Of fifteen legislators interviewed in person, nine stated that their interest in politics had originated during their childhood and continued throughout their life.

[4] Out of fifteen legislators questioned on this subject, five indicated that their political interest was the result of their direct political participation.

[5] Heinz Eulau **et al.**, "The Political Socialization Of American State Legislators," **Midwest Journal of Political Science, III** (May, 1959), 188-206.

[6] **Ibid.**, p. 191.

[7] **Ibid.**, p. 192.

[8] **Ibid.**

[9] **Ibid.**, p. 193.

[10] Roderick Bell, "The Determinants of Psychological Involvement in Politics: A Causal Analysis," **Midwest Journal of Political Science**, XIII (May, 1969), 251.

[11] Eulau **et al., op. cit.**, p. 194.

[12] **Ibid.**

[13] **Ibid.**, p. 200.

[14] William J. Keefe and Morris S. Ogul, **The American Legislative Process: Congress and the States** (Englewood Cliffs, N.J.: Prentice-Hall Inc., 1968), p. 101.

[15] John D. Parker, "Classifications of Candidates' Motivation for First Seeking Office," **Journal of Politics**, XXXIV (Feb., 1972), 270.

[16] **Ibid.**

[17] **Ibid.**

[18] **Ibid.**

[19] **Ibid.**

[20] Lester Seligman **et al., Patterns of Recruitment: A State Chooses its Lawmakers** (Chicago: Rand McNally, 1974), p. 83.

[21] **Ibid.**

[22] **Ibid.**, p. 85.

[23] **Ibid.**, p. 7

[24] **Ibid.**

[25] **Ibid.**

[26] **Ibid.**

[27] **Ibid.**

[28] Lester G. Seligman, "Political Recruitment and Party Structure: A Case Study." **American Political Science Review**, LV (March, 1961), 84.

[29] Seligman **et al., Patterns of Recruitment . . .** 30.

[30] V.O. Key, Jr., **American State Politics** (New York: Alfred A. Knopf, 1956), p. 271.

[31] However, of thirty-eight legislators consulted, only five were actively recruited by their party. Three were Republicans and two were Democrats.

[32] Key, **op. cit.**

[33] Of Thirty-six legislators questioned, seventeen received no help whatsoever, fourteen received some organizational help, three received some financial assistance — in the general election only, none for the primaries.

[34] According to the 1970 U.S. Census, Oakland is the wealthiest county in Michigan.

[35] Lester Seligman, **Recruiting Political Elites** (New York: General Learning Press, 1971), p. 14.

[36] **Ibid.**

[37] Thomas R. Dye, **Politics in States and Communities** (Englewood Cliffs, N.J.: Prentice-Hall Inc., 1969), p. 113.

[38] Duane Lockard, "The State Legislator," **State Legislatures in American Politics,** ed. Alexander Heard (Englewood Cliffs, N.J.: Prentice-Hall., 1966), p. 112.

[39] Frank J. Sorauf, **Political Parties in the American System** (Boston: Little, Brown and Co., 1964), p. 127.

[40] **Ibid.,** pp. 127-128.

[41] **Ibid.**

[42] Thomas R. Dye, **Politics in States and Communities** (Englewood Cliffs, N.J.: Prentice-Hall, Inc., 1973), p. 149.

[43] **Ibid.**

[44] Thomas R. Dye, "State Legislative Politics," **Politics in the American States,** ed. Herbert Jacob and Kenneth Vines(Boston: Little, Brown and Co., 1965), pp. 188-9.

CHAPTER V

THE COMMITTEE SYSTEM

In the Michigan legislature, it is within the standing committees that the most important legislative work is accomplished. As one legislator succinctly phrased it, "That's where the members really dog it and that's where the work is." It is in committee that a member is able to specialize and develop his expertise in a specific area. As a result of this assumption of knowledge, the full House or Senate will generally support the recommendations of a standing committee.

One legislator gives his impression of the position committees occupy in the following excerpt:

> The committees are the vital part of the legislature. If you don't get committee support, your legislative program is in jeopardy. There's kind of an unwritten rule that you follow the recommendation of the committee. You may debate the committee suggestions. You may try to alter some of their suggestions. But you generally accept — unless you're opposed to the idea completely. You generally accept their ideas.

In the Senate, it is the Committee on Committees that makes appointments to the various standing committees in the upper chamber.[1] The Committee on Committees is composed of the majority leader and five additional Senators who are appointed by the majority caucus. All appointments must be approved by a majority vote of the Senate. The first Senator named to a committee is its chairman. The chairman is always a member of the majority party.

After the election in November, the Senators receive a form from the office of the Secretary of Senate which requires the members of the Senate to indicate to which committees they would prefer to be assigned. When the Senate meets, the parties caucus, and it is in the caucus that the decisions as to which committees the various members will sit on, is made. The Committee on Committees will then meet and, in general, will accept the recommendations of the party caucus. After the Committee on Committees makes a final determination regarding committee assignments, it must be ratified by the full Senate. It is very rare for the Senate to reject the final judgment of the Committee on Committees. One Senator stated: "I don't recall a case where the recommendation of the Committee on Committees was rejected on the Senate floor." Another Senator explains the process in a little more detail in the following passage:

> The majority leader actually contacts the minority leader and indicates what the procedures would be under the rule. Then the Committee on

Committees sits down . . . and the minority leader and the majority leader are on that committee. Then they decide how these positions should be held. It's done very harmoniously.

In the House, it is the Speaker who assigns individuals to the various standing committees in the lower chamber.[2] Like their counterparts in the Senate, House members receive a questionnaire which requests the members to indicate the five committees which they would prefer. Most House members serve on three or four committees concurrently. After the questionnaires are returned, the Speaker of the House and his staff assemble to determine placement of the members of the House on the various standing committees. The Speaker will usually meet with the minority leader and consider his recommendations before reaching any final decisions. Some insight into committee assignments is provided by this excerpt from an interview with a House member:

Some meetings are held between the two party leaders in the House. Cliff Smart [minority leader] and Bill Ryan [Speaker of the House] sit down and Bill says: "I want him on Appropriations and I want him on Taxation." . . . Those kinds of accommodations are made, and sometimes the accommodations aren't possible so that's lashed out. Ryan says; "I don't want him on Taxation. I don't want him back on Labor; he just made trouble all the time he was there . . . We're not going to have a trouble-maker on that committee" . . . But you've got to understand that the Speaker is elected by his caucus and therefore, it behooves the Speaker to try and be fair to every member. It's not one of those situations where you can say to a member who has been a consistent thorn in your side as Speaker or as party leader: "No, I'm not going to give you that choice committee assignment because" whatever reason [sic] . . . He's got to have that guy's vote when it gets right down to the nitty-gritty on the floor. If a sufficient number of Democrats were unhappy with their caucus' choice of Speaker, they could join up with the Republicans and elect somebody else. That has happened.

The state party organization plays a modest role in the determination of committee assignments. Essentially, its role is an advisory one. The following is a description of the state party organization's part in this particular legislator's assignment to a standing committee:

Very minimal — a very minimal role. I think an advisory role . . . For example, when I went up, I'm sure there were some 'phone calls between the state party Chairman and Bill Ryan in terms of my request for the Elections Committee . . . So I talked to McNeely [the Democratic state party Chairman at that time] about that . . . and told him I wanted it and told him I was going to ask for it and I'd appreciate anything he could do to help me get it. And I got it. I have to assume that he was consulted on that one. But I think that's the extent of it. I mean, it's an advisory kind of role that they play, not a direct role.

Nor do interest groups play a significant role in the committee assignment process. This, however, was not always the case in the Michigan legislature, as this state Senator relates:

Years ago in this Legislature, they [interest groups] pretty much called the shots. The insurance lobby would practically name the chairman of the Insurance Committee, and name the members. The Farm Bureau, which is a tremendous political power, would practically name who went on Appropriations, who went on Agriculture and Taxation.

When asked about the role of interest groups in the committee assignment process today, the legislators had the following responses:

No, none that I know of. And if they did, I certainly would object.

If they do, it's very subtle. I would say it would be minimal.

They may play a small role. I don't think they play a significant role.

The truly decisive factors that determine on which committee a member will serve are: his own personal preference, his seniority, and his ability or degree of expertise. As one legislator phrased it: "First comes preference of the individual, and then, where there's a dispute, normally seniority." According to another legislator, committee assignments are made in the following way:

They look at your background very strongly. . . But I think, like everything else, the senior member is going to get his committee assignment choices where the junior member may not get all of his choices. They'll probably try to slot him in where they feel he's best qualified or where they need another Democratic body or another Republican body. So I think background has a good deal to do with it, but seniority probably has a good deal to do with it also.

Committees exist for the purpose of enabling the legislators in the House and in the Senate to develop expertise in specialized areas. An essential factor in this development is the need for the committees to have adequate staff assistance.[3] Here are three assessments of the degree of expertise engendered by the committees in Michigan's state legislature:

They do build up expertise; there's no question about it. Certainly, new members, when they are assigned to a committee [unless they come out of the field to begin with], are, let's say, a little bit just plain baffled at first. But, for example, the Committee on Taxation — you work for that committee for a period of years and you just have to absorb some expertise within the field of taxation. And the same is true of Education. Of course, all our committees do have very capable staff assistance. And, of course, the departments work with us very closely . . . the Department of Revenue, and certainly different tax divisions of the state, or all other departments. So the expertise is built up within the Committee system.

All of my life I had heard that everybody in the legislature is a dolt. They knew absolutely nothing. And when I got up there, I was amazed . . . I have never met a more knowledgeable group of men in my life than I've met right here in Lansing . . . You go to a committee meeting — I don't care what committee meeting it is — and everyone there is knowledgeable. They know the bill they're talking about — widely divergent views on what they should do with that bill. But I was amazed to find the calibre of people here that I did.

I'm from a very rural district. It's got a lot of agriculture in it. I'm chairman of the Committee on Agriculture. I even lived in a rented red brick Victorian farmhouse for seven years until just this summer — never farmed. I don't know anything about farming really, at all . . . I don't really think that's so important. It may sound strange, but I don't really think that's so important. I think what is important is that, if you are an intelligent person basically, and you have common sense, and you are practical and pragmatic, and you're easy to get along with, and you're objective — I think that you could fill almost any position on a legislative committee that you might be asked to fill, particularly the chairmanship. And I think, of course, as time goes on and you become more and more familiar with the field of study in which you're involved, . . . obviously you are going to get more efficient and you develop an expertise and you'll be more effective.

The selection as to which committee should consider each bill is determined by the presiding officer in each house. However, it is not always the obvious choice. Jurisdiction is not the sole criterion for determining where a bill should go. Many times the individual who introduces a bill will have a preference of one committee over another in the placement of his bill, and this is considered in making a final decision. In the Senate, it is generally the secretary of the Senate who designates which committee will consider a bill. However, the Lieutenant Governor, being the presiding officer of the Senate, can play a role here if he so desires. Usually, the reference of a bill to a committee is routine. If a member of the Senate objects to the placement of a bill in a particular committee he has two options. In the first case, a Senator may choose to work discreetly, behind the scene, and approach the Senate leadership directly to present his objections and/or preferences. To use the words of one Senator: "If there is someone who wishes a bill to go to another committee because it is questionable whether it should go to the one or the other, he will go to the secretary, or maybe the majority leader, and say he thinks the bill should be in X committee, rather than Y committee, and usually there's no problem." The second option involves the overt action of a Senator, in that he will present his objections on the floor of the Senate before his colleagues, and state openly that he feels a particular bill ought to go to a committee other than that to which it was assigned. To quote: "Most of the time, if you're interested in it going to a particular committee and that's where it should go . . . if there's some reasonable relationship to that committee, and not a particularly hot kind of thing, you won't have any trouble." If there is still some dispute, the full Senate is the final arbiter, by a majority vote. That is something which occurs rarely, perhaps once in a year.

In the area of committee assignments, the Governor is able to exercise some influence. According to one legislator: "Let's say the Governor wants to kill a bill. Well, it's easy enough for him just to tell the Lieutenant Governor 'this is the committee I want it to go to' because he and the chairman are buddy-buddy."

In the Michigan House it is the Speaker of the House who determines which committee will consider a bill. There must, however, be a relationship between the bill and the committee to which it is assigned. There is some latitude in referring a bill to a committee, and the membership of the House has some input into the assignment process. One Representative expressed the members' position thusly:

> If you author a bill and you go to the Speaker and explain to him you think it should go to a certain committee because, perhaps, you are afraid it will go to a committee where it would not get proper consideration. Usually, if you have a good reason to request a bill go to a certain committee, the Speaker will give it good consideration. So you have a little leeway.

Technically, if the Speaker assigns a bill to a committee and there is an objection by a member of the House, the member may have the bill re-routed if he can persuade a majority of the House to support him. In reality, there is little likelihood of such an occurrence.

> I don't know of a single instance where a bill did not go where the Speaker wanted it to go. Early in my legislative career, I tried to re-route the abortion bill. It came over from the Senate. The Speaker sent it to a very unfriendly committee. I wanted to send it to a friendlier committee. I got about thirty-one votes [out of 110].

Without exception, when asked to rank the various committees in their own chamber according to overall importance, the members of both the Senate and the House who either responded to the question-naire or were personally interviewed, placed their respective Appropriations Committee above all others. Any bill that requires a fairly large expenditure — over $30,000 — must be approved by the Appropriations Committee. Because of its large workload, Appropriations is the best staffed committee in the legislature. For many members, this is the only committee on which they serve, and no one sitting on Appropriations may serve on more than one additional committee. Although it is the most influential committee in both chambers, many legislators shun a position on Appropriations because of the enormous workload that is involved. What follows are three responses by some of the legislators who were interviewed, regarding the reasons for the primary import-ance of the Appropriations Committee.

> Any bill that comes before the Senate that has any fiscal implications what-soever, almost automatically gets sent down to the Appropriations Committee for a review before it comes out . . . In other words, they are a kind of a watchdog, as in the best respect they are . . . And they have a definite say on everything that happens. They have the greatest control over where the pork-barreling legislation can materialize and where it doesn't. If the people on the Appropriations Committee decide that the State Police post ought to go in one guy's district rather than another, that can make a difference. It's just got enormous power.

> Ninety percent of all legislation has to clear through the Appropriations Committee. Any bill that has the connotation of a dollar has to clear through

the House or Senate Appropriations Committee. So naturally, if you have the cash register, you are on the most important committee.

Appropriations is extremely expert . . . It has a really good staff on the Appropriations Committee. It's for that reason that the Governor, really and truly — in the state, on the budget — proposes and we dispose. We have a House fiscal agency, made up of some really capable people. And then we have the Senate fiscal agency.

Both the Senate and the House Fiscal Agencies are in important arm of the Appropriations Committee in each branch. The agencies employ about eight or ten people each. Their function is to research the bills which are under consideration by their respective Appropriations Committee, and to report these findings to the Committee.

While everyone questioned on the matter agreed that the Appropriations Committee was hard-working and very influential, not everyone was enthusiastic about its performance. There is a good deal of resentment toward the Committee, as one legislator implies in the following quotation from one of the interviews:

Let me be very blunt and frank with you. . . . Any bill that is complicated, any bill that has fiscal overtones to it — those bills tend to find their way into the Appropriations Committee. So that, in my opinion, to much too large extent the Appropriations Committee becomes the final arbitrator. You will pass a bill out of the Education Committee, for example. It cost money; it's got to go through Appropriations. So, they don't simply say "yes there's enough money" or "no, there's not enough money." They rewrite the bill. And they do it in both the Senate and the House.

Even some of the members of the Appropriations Committee admit to this practice of rewriting bills with which they disagree. As one member said: "Very often we will rewrite a bill — substantially even — because of our philosophy on that bill. It's wide open once it gets down here."

With the exception of the Appropriations Committees, most of the legislators who were interviewed expressed the belief that the other committees were inadequately staffed. However, when asked to compare the present committee staffs with those of previous years, all agreed that there had been a definite improvement over the years. Three legislators explained their views of the staffing of the various committees in the following quotations:

The Appropriations Committee has a large staff researching the cost of things, you know. They call it the Fiscal Agency. But I think most committees do not have adequate staff. They need more help. We rely somewhat on our legislative service bureau, where research is done. But they're so busy drafting bills and so on, that they don't have much time to do the necessary research.

The Appropriations Committee is well staffed, but no other committee in the House has more than a single staff person — usually a young guy or girl, usually a student going for a masters or a doctorate degree. They're rarely around more than a year or two, and then they're gone.

Now, even though Michigan is in the vanguard of states that have become more progressive and have improved their tools a little the last decade, we still lag. Now here, for instance, in the Senate, let's take my Committee on Agriculture and Consumer Affairs. I have a committee clerk and she takes the minutes and handles the meeting, technically — passes out cards, and keeps the bills in order, and does all this stuff. But she doesn't have the background, sometimes, to lend technical staff assistance. That is not her purpose.

In describing the operation of committees in either the Senate or the House, most committees do not use a sub-committee system. Only the largest of the committees employ such a system. It is not surprising, therefore, that the Appropriations Committees use subcommittees most often of all the committees, 'though not exclusively. The Committee on Taxation and the Judiciary Committee also use the sub-committee system to a lesser degree. The chairman of a committee appoints the sub-committee chairman. Generally speaking, the recommendations of the sub-committee are accepted by the full committee. When asked if there were many sub-committees in the Michigan legislature, one member made this reply:

Not really as many as there should be. Taxation has some, Judiciary has some, and Appropriations, of course, has a large number. But other than that, I don't think so. Occasionally some of the committees will appoint a short term committee to study a particular bill or something and report back to the full committee. But very rarely. We haven't used that structure which, I think, would be an ideal way to handle it more effectively.

Under the Michigan constitution, it is required that committee hearings be open to the public. It is necessary for the committee to notify the public in advance, of the hearings and the subjects to be considered at each hearing (Art. IV, Sec. 17). According to Article IV, Section 20, the hearings are closed to the public only as a matter of public security. Public hearings are an important source of information. They are especially important to those committees who are short on staff, as they enable the work of the committees to be opened to the public. Sometimes the hearings take place in an area that would be affected by a bill that is under consideration by a committee. The principal advantage of the hearings is the greater access they provide to the committees by the public at large, and not just the well-organized interest groups. One legislator describes committee hearings in this excerpt.:

Normally . . . you hold public hearings because you're fishing: you want information, you want inputs. Now, it's no problem if you're talking about a bill that is going to regulate an industry or something. It's no problem to get the man from Consumers or Detroit Edison to appear before your committee. Well, that's their job. They're in Lansing all the time. Those are the guys that want to take you out to lunch, and this kind of stuff. The problem is getting out and getting input from people — just plain people. Just plain people do not attend committee meetings in Lansing and therefore, if you want to hear from them, the only way you're going to do it is to go where they are and publicize your coming.

Not all legislators share the enthusiasm of the preceding committee member. Although no one questions the value of public hearings, many legislators are not totally committed to these hearings, as the following quotation indicates:

It does give the public a chance to air their feelings on the proposed bill, either in opposition or in support. Or they might make a suggestion that would improve the bill. And I would say you'd have to continue with public hearings, 'cause in many cases, it's the only time that the public can find out what it's all about. Because again, in newspaper reporting you don't go into detail. You tell the spectacular, the sensational, and many times the spectacular and the sensational are not even a part of the bill.

Thus, open hearings have two important functions: they provide the members of the committee with an awareness of the sentiments of the various communities, and secondly, the public hearings enlighten the members of the community in regard to the true nature of the bill under consideration. Of course, most committee hearings are held in Lansing — for very practical reasons. The practice of public hearings at the local level is too cumbersome a technique to utilize as a matter of course. It is difficult to arrange meetings for routine bills outside of the state capital in Lansing. Therefore, this technique is reserved for controversial matters, where the legislators are anxious to test public sentiment.

When meetings and hearings are scheduled to be held outside of Lansing, the customary procedure is to issue press releases in advance of the hearing. When the public attends a meeting, the committee clerk will be at the door to greet the people and to pass out blank cards. Those who wish to speak at the meeting write their names and addresses and the amount of time they will require on the card. They also indicate whether they are in support of or in opposition to the bill in question. The cards are then returned to the committee clerk.

Once the fact-finding phase has been completed in and/or outside of Lansing, the next step in the passage of a bill is the debate on the bill itself, within the committee. It is during this phase that the various compromises are made, in order to get a bill which will be approved by a majority of legislators. The average committee receives approximately two hundred bills each session. The committee has several options: it may report a bill out of committee as is; it may report the bill out with amendments; it may report a substitute bill; it may choose to take no action on a bill, and thus let it die in committee. The following is one legislator's description of this process:

· If you're sponsoring a bill, the first thing you want to do is get it into a friendly committee. The second thing you want to do is get to that committee chairman and make sure it's on the agenda. The next thing you want to do is be there the day they discuss the bill. So that in addition to attending your own committees, you will also be hopping in and out of these other committees that are hearing your bills. You make your presentation. You tell them the merits of your bill, why you think it's good legislation. You respond to any questions they ask. If somebody, say it's a Republican and I'm a Democrat, you know says well, would you accept this or that amendment. You look around the committee and you count the votes. And if you think you've got the votes, you reject the amendment. But if you look around and you don't have the votes, you say yes, I think we can live with that amendment.

In most cases, once a bill has been reported out of a committee, it is accepted on the floor of the House or Senate. Usually, the author of a bill acts as the floor manager for that bill. However, if the bill is of a technical and complex nature, then the chairman of the committee will respond to questions on the floor and will see to it that the bill is accepted. When the legislators were asked about the number of bills passed on the floor of the House or Senate after their acceptance by a committee, one legislator estimated "that eighty percent of the bills that hit the floor are passed." Another legislator explained this high rate of passage in the following way:

As I indicated, from my committee we have never lost a bill. I think the reason is that we thoroughly review it, thoroughly check with the opponents and see whether there's any strong opposition. If there is, how we can overcome it. How we can amend the bill without damaging the reasons for the legislation. In that way, I think we've been quite successful.

Those bills which are of a controversial nature usually go to a conference committee in order to work out the differences between the Senate and House versions. Three members are selected from each chamber. In the Senate, the Lieutenant Governor selects the conference committee members. In the House, the Speaker appoints three members to serve on the conference committee. In each chamber, two of the appointed members represent the majority and the remaining member is chosen from the minority party. All appropriations bills go into conference committees. About ten percent of the remaining bills are sent to conference committees. In general, the sponsor of the bill will be appointed to the conference committee, and usually someone from the original committee that developed the bill. In the House, the Speaker may assign himself to a conference committee if the bill under consideration is an important one. After the differences are ironed out, the bill is then returned to each house for final approval.

Besides its vital role in drafting legislation and improving upon legislation referred to it, and its role in developing the expertise of its members, the standing committee also has an oversight function. The committee can be an important tool in keeping the various executive agencies in check. When asked about this oversight function, one legislator stated: "We do what we can. This has always been one of our real hangups as to the authority a legislature has after an appropriation has been made." Another legislator explained his view in more detail:

> I don't think the legislature is a very effective check on the executive. If it should be, it isn't . . . I think state government has gotten so large that we have a difficult problem. We're going into this program budgeting, and this is just going to absolutely blow the minds of everybody in the legislature because nobody is going to understand it. . . Now, we've got twelve people over in the House Fiscal Agency who are going to try to walk through this thing and try to figure it out. But I think it's going to be very difficult, very difficult. And you've got executive branch agencies which promulgate administrative rules which we have very little check over.

During the course of the interviews and other conversations with members of the legislature, it became apparent that many legislators — both Senate and House members — were unfamiliar with the word oversight, and were not aware of that particular function as an aspect of their responsibilities or duties. The only committee in either chamber which is capable of performing the oversight function in the Appropriations Committee. Yet this committee does not appear to carry out this function with any frequency or, when they do, it is without depth. For the most part, the committees in the Senate and House accept the word of the executive agencies in regard to how they are functioning. In addition to their own investigation, the committees also rely on the annual report of the Auditor-General and on constituent mail to inform them of any inefficiency or incompetancy in the administrative agencies.

The chairmanship of a committee is a responsible position which carries with it the potential for a great deal of influence. The more important a committee is, the greater is the responsibility and influence which rests with the chairman of that committee. Consequently, the position of committee chairman is sought after by most legislators. In the upper chamber, it is the majority leader who appoints the chairman to each committee, while in the lower chamber, the Speaker of the House assigns the chairmanships. The following is a description of this process by one of the legislators:

> The Speaker appoints the chairman. He appoints the vice-chairman. This year [1972] because we had a fifty-eight to fifty-two margin in the House, but a very uneasy margin because at any given time there are at least four Democrats ready to bolt. . . So Ryan did something new this time. He ap-

pointed a committee chairman that would be a Democrat and he would
appoint a vice-chairman who's a Democrat, and then he would appoint
another vice-chairman, a Republican. So he gave it for each of those com-
comittees. Virtually all of them have a Republican vice-chairman, which
looks nice on that Republican letterhead when they mail stuff out. Ryan
felt he had to do it in order to maintain the alliance, placate the Republicans.

Another House member describes the process this way:

The Speaker makes that recommendation and there is a vice-chairman
which he also recommends. And there is a Republican vice-chairman which
Cliff Smart [minority leader] recommends to the Speaker, and the Speaker
recommends him. Now, officially, they are picked by the committee. But I
have never known of a committee not to, in effect, ratify what the Speaker
has announced is going to be.

In the Senate, there is a Committee on Committees which,
together with the majority leader, appoints the committee chairmen.
The procedure works in the following manner, according to two
members of the Senate:

The majority leader and the Committee on Committees would decide. On
the Republican side in the Senate, it's done very harmoniously. Now, in case
there is some opposition, then you have to take the whole problem to the
Republican caucus, which will have to make the decision.

Usually, over here, the way I've seen it done — at least under this majority
leader — is that the Committee on Committees, which is a joint committee
of leadership of the Senate Democratic Caucus and the Senate Republican
Caucus, determine the chairmanships.

Seniority plays a role in determining who is selected as committee
chairman. But as the following statements indicate, seniority is not the
sole criterion, nor is it even the most important one:

Oh, seniority is important, but you've got to realize that this body doesn't
have that much seniority. There's a lot of turnover. I'm in my third term in the
House now, and I suppose that my class who entered in '69 probably are just
at about the break-point between half who have been here before us and
half who have been here after us. . . So seniority is a factor, but it's pretty
easy to acquire seniority here reasonably rapidly because of the turnover.

Seniority does not play that big a part in the legislature. . . First of all, there's
a great turnover in the legislature, much more so than in Congress. You get
a big, big shift, and one man-one vote in 1964 wiped out just over half the
legislature. Then we've had a census since then, and redistricting this year,
and that's wiped out about twenty-five in the House. In the Senate, we didn't
have to run this year, but there'll be changes two years from now. Because
the legislature is more of a mobile body. It's like musical chairs and revolv-
ing doors . . . And because we are not so hidebound by tradition here, you
do have a greater flexibility in terms of chairmanships and who gets
what committee.

The appointment of committee chairmen partial to the Governor's
position on particular issues can be crucial in determining whether or

not the Governor's program will pass through the legislature. The legislators were questioned to see what role, if any, the Governor played in the appointment. This legislator's response represents a consensus of those interviewed: "No. The Lieutenant Governor used to serve on the Committee on Committees, but we felt he was part of the executive and not legislative, and he was removed." Thus, not only is the role of the Governor in the appointment process slight, but it has actually been reduced in the Senate, with the removal of his agent, the Lieutenant Governor, from the Committee on Committees. As long as the House remains under the control of the Democrats, Governor Milliken's role will be minimal in the appointment of chairmen to committees in the House. The investigation of the Governor's role brought forth these comments from two legislators:

> There might be some casual conversation occasionally, but not from the standpoint of him directing who would be a chairman. He might have a recommendation, but that wouldn't happen very often.

> Oh, I think he can make a few suggestions. But I've been in caucus and his suggestions are just suggestions of a private citizen, as far as a caucus is concerned.

The most important factors in the assignment of an individual to the position of committee chairman seem to be, according to the information gathered from the interviews and questionnaires: experience, ability, and party loyalty. The following excerpts attest to this fact:

> Generally, the chairman of a committee is the chairman because he has had some previous experience in local government and is able to translate that into the committee he chairs. . . Some chairmen are there because nobody else wanted that particular chairmanship. By and large, they're there because they like that particular aspect of their work.

> The chairman, as a rule, is not a new member. The chairman would most likely have a great deal of experience. The Speaker appoints the chairman. I must give him credit. He usually appoints a person who has some background in that particular committee's work.

Because of the nineteen to nineteen split in 1972 and the fact that there were sixteen standing committees in the Senate, almost everyone could obtain a chairmanship. In the House, however, competition for the position of chairman is more avid, even though there are more standing committees than in the Senate. One method utilized to reduce the number of injured feelings was the institution of the position of vice-chairman. Thus, practically everyone in the House has some title that he can affix to his stationery letterhead.

Once an individual has attained the position of committee chairman, there are certain qualities he should possess in order for him to be particularly effective. To quote one legislator who is a House member, and another in the Senate:

> I think, first of all, the chairman has to be the kind of guy who can maintain the trust and the confidence of his committee members in both parties. The kind of fellow who, when a bi-partisan effort is required, can produce. . . I think a guy who is patient, because that does require patience, a guy who is fair so that everybody, regardless of their party, feels that they're getting a chance to speak on a bill, that they're getting their influence in, that they're being heard and treated fairly — those, I think, are probably the prime requirements.

> I think his ability to get along with not only the members of his committee but with the members of the Senate as a whole. His knowledge of the issues that come before his committee; the way he treats his committee and the respect that goes along with it that other members have for him; just being held as a person that they have complete faith and confidence and trust in — this makes it in my committee. And knowledge — knowledge is the key to power. I think those are things that make for an effective chairman. And a powerful chairman, if you want to use that expression.

The chairman of a standing committee has an impressive array of powers. He can virtually dictate whether a bill will survive or die in his committee. What follows are descriptions of some of the things a committee chairman can do, according to two legislators:

> Well, first of all he decides whether or not there is going to be a meeting of the committee, and where and when and what is discussed. What the agenda is going to be, what bills are we going to talk about, . . . if there is any staff person assigned to that committee — in reality they are assigned to the chairman and you usually find that aide working out of the chairman's office. So in terms of any research that is going to be done, the chairman plays a very direct role. . . If the Speaker wants a bill out, he's got to convince the chairman . . . If there's going to be any hearings on a bill, the chairman makes that decision — first: are there going to be public hearings; secondly: if so, where. He has a tremendous amount of authority in terms of that committee. If a bill were to come out of committee over his vote, it's very likely that if it got on the floor, if the chairman got up and spoke against the bill it would die, because he's looked upon as the expert guy. And usually, he's been around long enough to be able to put fifty-six votes together.

> Generally, the chairman can decide everything. The chairman can decide what bills are taken up, in what order, how long people get to speak, when the debate stops, whether the bill is going to be taken up again. He can decide whether he wants to put it to a vote. He can control the voting pattern almost around the table sometimes. I've had to play games with some of my committee members with amendment, and so forth, to get a bill out that I wanted out . . . There was a bill reported out . . . that I wanted but I couldn't get it out in the form I wanted it in. So I gigged [sic] and let it go out. I got the support of a committee member with one of his amendments in that I didn't like, but it was the only way I could get his vote to get it out on the floor. Then I went out on the floor and, with another committee member, we got the amendment taken off on the floor and passed it that way.

The chairman of a standing committee, then, is almost omnipotent. In many respects, he closely resembles a lord of a feudal fiefdom. Generally, he is a person with experience, knowledge and ability. He has almost absolute control over the life or death of a bill. He determines whether a bill will die in his committee or will be reported out as originally presented, with amendments, or completely altered. He, more than any other single individual, is responsible for the legislation that comes before the Governor for final approval.

In order to determine the effectiveness of a legislative committee system, certain criteria must be employed. These include: the rate of turnover, the importance of seniority, the number of standing committees in the legislature, the degree of specialization of standing committees, the ability of a committee to not report bills out, the extent to which committee recommendations are followed by the full House or Senate, whether or not committees meet in interim sessions, the size of committee staff, and whether the committee system performs an oversight function. It is these criteria which have been utilized in this paper to evaluate the Michigan legislature's committee system.

The rate of turnover in Michigan's legislature is fairly high. This is reflected in the committees. Between 1966 and 1971, Rosenthal noted that in such committees as Appropriations and Finance, there was a moderately high turnover in chairmanships.[4] The primary reason for this was the frequent change in the membership of the committees themselves. The rate of turnover in Michigan's assembly has declined since 1893.[5] However, it is still two to three times greater than in Congress.[6] A consequence of the high rate of turnover in the Michigan legislature is the difficulty the committees have in attaining a high degree of expertise in their specific domains. Although a committee chairman may be the senior committee member, it is possible that he may have only a few years of experience in that committee. It does not take too many years of legislative service to acquire some measure of seniority. It is not surprising, therefore, to find that the seniority factor is of limited use in the assignation of committee memberships — particularly the position of chairman. A legislator's preference and ability, as well as his seniority, are taken into consideration for committee placement.

The Michigan Legislature has a total of fifty-one standing committees — eighteen in the Senate and thirty-three in the House of Representatives. The study published by the Citizens Conference on State Legislatures has concluded that these figures are too high and has made the following recommendation:

Reduce the number of committees. Ideally, there should be from ten to fifteen committees in each house, parallel in jurisdiction. This would reduce the general complexity of the legislature and would permit reducing the number of committee assignments per member.[7]

With each legislative member serving on no more than three or four committees simultaneously, committee members are able to concentrate their attention and develop their expertise to the point where they can contribute effectively to the legislation confronting their committees.

The degree of specialization of the standing committees is not as high as it might be.

A description of the jurisdiction of committees should be contained in the rules of both houses, and assignment of bills should be made in accord with the jurisdiction of committees as described in rules.[8]

Because committee jurisdiction is not clearly set forth, responsibility for some legislation may overlap. Both the Senate and House Appropriations Committees receive, for consideration and action, all legislation involving sums of money in excess of $30,000, after these bills have been reported out of their original committees. This is the most obvious illustration of the overlapping of committee responsibility.

"A committee system performs less well if a large proportion of bills referred to it are given favorable action."[9] In Michigan, standing committees are not required to report out all bills. Thus, the committees are able to focus their time and efforts on those matters they deem to be most essential. Once a bill has been reported out of a committee, it is unusual to find that the committee's recommendation is not followed. Because the Michigan legislature has unlimited session days each year, the committees are able to meet on a fairly regular basis when the legislature convenes. In addition, the committees can meet during legislative recesses. The result is that the committees can meet frequently and thereby provide the members with time to thoroughly examine the legislation which concerns their committees.

Rosenthal has stated that "of all the resources standing committees draw on for their task of formulating and controlling state policies and programs, staff is probably the most important one."[10] It has been pointed out in the legislative interviews that adequate staffing is regarded as a problem by most committee members. The legislators view the Appropriations Committees as having sufficient staff assistance. However, rarely does any other legislative committee have more than a single staff member. This condition reduces the competancy of the standing committees. Rosenthal warns that an increase in staff assistance will not, in and of itself, necessarily reduce the workload of a committee or its members.[11] It is conceivable that a larger committee staff would uncover additional problems, alternatives, or opportunities and in so doing, actually increase the committee's work.

An important function of standing committees is an ability to evaluate the programs of the executive branch, in terms of compliance with the law, program efficiency, and fiscal responsibility.[12] The oversight function is the principal way in which a legislature maintains independent access to information and the capacity to analyze this information. If a legislature is to be independent of the executive branch, then the oversight function must be possessed and utilized. Yet by the legislators' own admissions, this function is not properly carried out by the Michigan legislature's standing committees. In fact, many legislators did not fully understand what the oversight function involved, as they reported in their interviews. To a large extent, the legislators rely upon executive agencies to provide them with reports on the efficiency and propriety of the executive branch of Michigan's government.

---

[1] Ferris E. Lewis, **State and Local Government in Michigan** (Boston: Allyn and Bacon, Inc., 1965), p. 38.

[2] **Ibid.,** p. 41.

[3] John C. Wahlke, "Organization and Procedure," **State Legislatures in American Politics,** ed. Alexander Heard (Englewood Cliffs, N.J.: Prentice-Hall, Inc. 1966), p. 142.

[4] Alan Rosenthal, **Legislative Performance in the States: Exploration of Committee Behavior** (New York: the Free Press, 1974), pp. 178-179.

[5] David Ray, "Membership Stability in Three State Legislatures, 1893-1969," **American Political Science Review,** LXVIII (March, 1974), 107.

[6] Kenneth T. Palmer, **State Politics in the United States** (New York: St. Martin's Press, 1972), p. 66.

[7] The Citizens Conference on State Legislatures, **State Legislatures: An Evaluation of Their Effectiveness, The Complete Report by the Citizens Conference on State Legislatures** (New York: Praeger Publishers, Inc., 1971), p. 208.

[8] **Ibid.,** p. 209.

[9] Rosenthal, **op. cit.,** p. 18.

[10] **Ibid.,** p. 146.

[11] **Ibid.,** p. 189.

[12] Citizens Conference on State Legislatures, **op. cit.,** p. 208.

CHAPTER VI

LEGISLATIVE LEADERSHIP AND INPUTS

The Constitution of the state of Michigan has invested the Governor of the state with many legislative powers. He prepares the state budget and submits it to the legislature for approval (Art. V, Sec. 18). He has an item veto (Art. V, Sec. 19). It takes the vote of two-thirds of both houses of the legislature to override the Governor's veto. The Governor may convene a special session of the legislature and may determine what subject or subjects are to be discussed at this special session (Art. V, Sec. 15). In addition to these important constitutional benefits, the Governor is also an important initiator of legislation. In his State of the State address, the Governor generally presents his program. Bills are then drafted by his administrative agencies and passed down to the legislature for consideration. The combination of all these functions have made the Governor one of the most important influences on the legislature. And the constitutional advantages with which he is endowed serve to enhance his influence over the legislative body of the Michigan government. The following quotations are representative of the way in which many Michigan legislators perceive the Governor's influence upon the legislature. The present Governor of the state, William Milliken, is a Republican, and partisanship may color the perceptions of the oppositions somewhat. The two excerpts which follow are taken from interviews with Democratic legislators, where they discuss the Governor's role in the legislature and the influence he bears — as they perceive it:

> He has his hand in everything. If he's a good governor, if he's a powerful governor. . . I personally don't think he's very influential. The fact that he has a good legislative record is a tribute to us in meeting our responsibilities. I kind of laugh at the way the press has glorified him, as how Milliken gets tough. That's a gag. Many times some of us are faced with the responsibility of embarrasing the Governor or doing the right thing. And what we hope to do eventually is do the right thing.

> It's been very rare that we've had the Governor and both houses of the legislature from the same party, and so that produces its own frictions. Currently [1972] of course, the Governor is a Republican, the Senate is Republican, and the House is democratic. And so there are people in the Governor's office whose job it is to work with the legislature. Their major effort is probably concentrated toward the Republican members, but on those areas where there is an opportunity to work together, they also work with us. And I've had, frankly, some good experiences with guys like Jim Kellogg and Dr. Bill Taylor in the Governor's office. . . People have said that "politics is the art of the possible," but basically, it's the art of compromise. You never quite get the whole loaf. Very rarely do you get that. And so we learn to work to get as much of the loaf as we can. And the Governor has that problem, as the executive leader of this state, to a much greater

degree than any of us as individual legislators do. And so his office, although it is an executive office, his office does play a significant role in the legislative process as well.

There can be no question that the office of Governor is indeed an an influential position. One Democratic legislator, when interviewed expressed some rather bitter sentiment about the advantages the Governor has in the press. Often it is the Governor who receives credit for legislation which the legislature has worked on and passed. This publicity advantage is another source of the Governor's influence. Many bills are drafted in the Governor's office. They are then given to sympathetic Republicans in leadership positions in the Senate or House, who then proceed to introduce the bill on the Governor's behalf. The two quotations which follow relate to the way in which members of his own party perceive the Governor's role in the legislature:

He submits the state of the state message and then he prepares the budget. That book looks like the telephone book and is our budget here. This baby has eleven-hundred-and-some pages. And then he submits special messages on everything. And he has every department in the executive branch of govern- ment suggest what legislation they think should be sponsored for the coming year. And then he has bills prepared on that, and he or his staff looks them over and decides which ones they want to endorse as executive bills. And they can get them prepared and sent over here for introduction. And they come through our minority office, and I don't know how many of them go over directly to the Democrats now. But they're peddled around. They get introduced. And then, of course, he has veto power. And he's got patronage in the districts. He's got a staff of liaison people that button-hole us and plead with us, and try to keep us in line on various things. So, he's got quite a lot of means to express himself.

Well, the Governor, being a Republican Governor, works closely with Republican leadership in both the House and the Senate. And we meet with him very often on major issues — maybe at his home for breakfast every Wednesday morning, or at other times. Sometimes it's the caucus that meets with him. He has, on his staff, liaison people who work with the entire legislature on legislation that he has a particular interest in.

It can thus be seen that the Governor plays a very important role in the initiation of legislation. He has a distinct advantage in that the entire executive branch is at his disposal to devise and draft legislation which the Governor desires. The legislature has neither the staff nor the expertise to compare with that of the Governor's office. The Governor maintains constant contact with the legislature. He meets with his party's leadership at regular intervals. He also keeps in touch with the leadership of the Democratic party in the legislature. When the Governor himself cannot contact the leadership personally, he has his liaison people maintain contact for him. His influence is considerable. In fact, among some of his Republican colleagues in the legislature, there is a certain amount of resentment toward the Governor for what the legislators consider to be his interference in the legislative process, and also because of all the advantages inherent in the executive branch. One example of a situation which causes some resentment is the news conference. When the Governor calls the reporters in for a news conference, he makes the front pages of the papers, while when a legislator calls for a news conference, he is fortunate if the newsmen are present. The legislators did indicate that some of their feelings were dependent upon the personality of the man in office. Some chose to compare the present Governor, William Milliken with his predecessor, Governor George Romney. They noted vast differences in the styles of these two individuals. Romney was very strong and forceful. He had been known to pound on a table and even to grab hold of a legislator by his lapels or to shake him — in order to make his point. Milliken is regarded to be more of a gentleman, and is inclined to use a softer approach in persuading his colleagues to support his point of view.

The most important member of the Michigan legislature itself is the Speaker of the House. Commensurate with his importance, the Speaker has the largest staff of any individual or committee in the House or Senate. He has some twenty-five people working under him.[1] This staff includes secretaries and messengers. Some of the functions performed by the Speaker's staff include providing administrative services to all the members of the House, regardless of their party affiliation. The staff also contains a section devoted to bill analysis. This group must analyze each and every bill introduced in the legislature. It must determine what problem the bill is directed at solving, the need for the legislation, and the priority of any given piece of legislation.[2]

The Speaker of the House also serves as the caucus leader of the majority party in the House. It is the Speaker who calls the House to order and who maintains the proper decorum and procedure. He decides questions of order, refers bills to the appropriate committees, makes appointments to the committees, recognizes who shall speak from among the members of the House, and votes on all questions.

The Speaker of the House at the time the interviews were conducted was William Ryan. Each Speaker brings with him, to his office, his own particular style. In the case of Speaker Ryan, that style included a tremendous ability to negotiate with others. Both Democratic and Republican perceptions and evaluations of the Speaker are remarkable for their consistency, particularly in regard to the role which his colleagues felt he ought to play and that which, in fact, he did play. to quote:

Although I don't agree with Ryan's philosophy, I think Ryan does a hell of a job as Speaker of the House. You very seldom see him on the podium. I don't think he should be there. If he is, he's ineffective. He has no power up there except to rap people down. I think we're fortunate in one way, having a man like Ryan as Speaker. As I say, I don't agree with him, but we're fortunate in the fact that Ryan is a born negotiator. It's his whole life. And if we had a guy that wouldn't negotiate, with the votes he's got we'd be in trouble. He'll negotiate on any damned point you want to negotiate on. I don't care what it is.

Bill Ryan is just — you know. They should have sent him to the Paris Peace Conference. He's a fantastic negotiator. He's patient. He can outwit everyone. Everyone else wants to go home and Bill will wait, and wait, and wait, and wear you down — a master negotiator. I've seen him negotiate on a tax bill with Governor Romney. He stole everything but the buttons off the Governor's shirt . . . He used labor negotiator techniques. He used to be a labor negotiator, before I came up here. Just fantastic!

Part of the Speaker's success seems to be attributable to the amount of time he is willing to devote to his job. Ryan is a bachelor and therefore, does not have family responsibilities to encumber him. He lives austerely; he has a one-room apartment across the street from the State Capitol which even lacks its own bathroom. His office, however, is more impressive. His office and staff require three rented floors in an office building across from the Capitol Building. Several legislators have remarked that Ryan is probably the second most important elected official in Michigan. One legislator commented on the Speaker's influence:

Nothing happens without the Speaker's approval. He works through the various committee chairmen to carry out his mandates. He gets his own way about all the time. He wears down the Governor. Well, the Governor has got a few other things to do and he spends so much time at it. But Ryan — he's got unlimited time, seven days a week. It makes no difference to him. He'd just wear the opposition down . . . What he wants, he gets . . . He's at least number two man in the state, if not number one man when it comes to determining what's going to happen.

The key, then, to the Speaker's influence seems clearly to be the amount of time he is willing to spend bargaining and negotiating. This, in effect, enables him to maneuver legislation through the House. The fact that he spends less time presiding on the floor of the House frees him to work at getting the legislation through. However, the Speaker is not without some criticism. One legislator, from Speaker Ryan's own party, felt that the Speaker should be more innovative, that he should utilize his large staff to develop a complete program to represent the Democratic party's ideals. Ryan was critized for working on bills piecemeal. Yet in the main, Ryan was respected and admired by most of the legislators — Democrats and Republicans alike.

In the Senate, the Lieutenant Governor is the presiding officer. The 1963 Michigan constitution provides, in Article V, Section 25, that:

"The Lieutenant Governor shall be president of the senate, but shall have no vote unless they be equally divided. He may perform duties requested of him by the Governor, but no power vested in the Governor shall be delegated." His role in the Senate is limited. At one time, the Lieutenant Governor used to serve on the Committee on Committees, but as previously mentioned, this function was taken away because he was perceived to be a part of the executive branch, rather than a true member of the Senate. While technically he is required to preside over the Senate, in fact he is there only about half of the time. The Lieutenant Governor is invited to attend his party's caucuses in the Senate, but he rarely appears. The role of the Lieutenant Governor, then, is limited both by practice and by statute.

When the Lieutenant Governor is not presiding over the Senate, this function is taken over by the President Pro Tempore. The following is an excerpt from an interview with a member of the Senate in which the role of the President Pro Tempore is described:

> The President Pro Tempore is elected by the Senate Republicans and Democrats — a combination of the two. Obviously, the majority party recommends who they want, but he is the highest elected official in the Senate. And my role and function is to, first of all, see that the Senate runs smoothly, orderly, that things proceed, to gain the respect of the members, judgments which I have to make, decisions for the chair. I have not been over-ruled yet, by the body when I've made a decision. I think the purpose is to gain the respect of the members, so that when the chair says something, he means it. And they know it and respond accordingly..

Yet it is the majority leader in the Senate who has the most influence among the Senators. To a large extent, the Governor acts through the majority leader — when they are of the same political party. The majority leader may act as a conduit for the Governor's programs. One Senator described the majority leader's role thusly:

> I would say a very important role in this Senate because he is the Governor's representative with the Republican Senators. He does try to push the bills through that the Governor is interested in. And he still tries to maintain a good rapport with his colleagues in the Senate, and that's difficult because he generally doesn't get full accord from the Senators as to what he is trying to do for the Governor. He tries to maintain harmony between the two political parties and tries to keep the programs moving forward.

The majority leader is also the caucus leader for the majority party, which was the Republican party in 1972. He is influential in determining the agenda for the daily Senate workload. "He moves bills up and down the calendar, provided he gets at least minimal co-operation from the Democrats. He calls the shots on the floor of the Senate, making motions to adjourn and recess, and he really is the power on the floor."

76

The minority leader is elected by his party's caucus. He has important input regarding which of his party's members will sit on which particular committees. He is also responsible for attempting, to the greatest possible degree, to assure that his party's program gets through the Senate. Three legislators offer the following interpretations of the role of the minority leader in the Senate:

> The minority leader has, I think, a dual role: first, he is the leader of the party, or the minority party; as the minority leader he is also the leader of, let's say, the loyal opposition — to point out defects or faults in legislation and, certainly, to effectuate compromises. So again, . . . the people are the benefactors.

> The minority leader should watch sharp and try to salvage as much as he can out of what goes on. And try to see to it that we have as good an attendance record as possible when committee meetings are in session. Keep our folks here. and every once in a while a situation develops where, for two or three hours, we've got floor control. That is, we'd have more of our party on the floor than they would. And then he could determine what amendments are going to be adopted and what ones weren't. And so, if our minority group is going to be effective, they have to be reasonably harmonious and informed on what the issues are.

> Well, the minority leader has to maximize the strength of the minority, certainly. And then, to negotiate too. To try to secure as much of their caucuses, whatever their positions might be on any legislation that might pass.

It is in the caucus that the minority leader explains the issues, presents the intentions of the opposition party, and determines what their own response should be. He endeavors to achieve as near a unanimous decision as possible. Yet there are always a few legislators who, for reasons of conscience, philosophy, or constituent sentiment, will not accede to the party line. Usually that action is accepted with good grace, unless they are consistent naysayers. In the House and in the Senate during the 1972-73 session, the Republicans caucused about once a week, while the Democrats caucused on the average of once a month.

In general, there is a good deal of co-operation between the minority and majority leaders in the Senate, and between the minority leader and the Speaker in the House. This is due, in part, to the close divisions along party lines in the 1972 legislature. The parties cannot rely on all of their members to follow party policy all of the time. Therefore, in order to get their legislative programs through the legislature, the leaders must have the co-operation of both parties.

Another elective position of leadership in the legislature is the party whip. His principal function is to make sure the members are on the floor when a crucial vote comes up. The position also carries some prestige. Here are two descriptions of the role of the party whip in the Michigan state legislature:

> Well, the role they play is, frankly, an honorary one. It is something that looks good on your letterhead, this sort of thing. But there is a need for good floor management. The whip role should be to help take the nose count, make sure the votes are there on legislation, and back up the floor leader on parliamentary moves and so on. But they don't do it.

> Each of us is assigned ten legislators in the House. Our job is to see to it that they're accounted for, that they're present and particularly, that their views on important measures are known. If the Speaker wants to know today how we're going to vote on a controversial measure, we have to check each one of them out, ask them their position, are they going to be there, are they going to vote. Be a part of the leadership, to try to convince. If he's a suburbanite legislator, try to convince him that we need his vote to raise the city of Detroit income tax and also raise the tax of the non-resident. There are many, many functions. Hundreds of them. It depends on every bill, every day.

Another source of influence on the Michigan legislature is the interest groups. The most visible and, according to some of the legislators who were interviewed, probably the most influential lobbies are: the American Federation of Labor, or AFL; the United Automobile Workers, or UAW; the Michigan Educational Association, or MEA: the American Federation of Teachers; and the Michigan Farm Bureau. Surprisingly, the Automobile Industry was not mentioned by the legislators during the interviews — unless it was suggested to them. This, however, should not negate its influence, for as Keefe and Ogul have stated: "The best equipped lobbies tend to work silently."[3] When asked to discuss the influence of the Automobile Industry on the legislators, some asserted that this particular interest group was not as influential as it had been in the past. One legislator commented that the one man/one vote decision [Baker v. Carr, 369 U.S. 186 (1962)] has increased the role of labor, and it was believed that labor's growth has tended to serve as a counterforce against the Automobile Industry lobby. He went on:

> Labor is a powerful interest group. They maintain full-time lobbyists . . . The AFL maintains a full-time lobbyist . . . The Teamsters maintain a full-time guy . . . And they work together on some issues. And they work very close to each other on issues. And then someone is supporting an issue and the other could care less. That happens a lot.

One Republican legislator noted, rather bitterly, the close support that labor provides the Democratic party. Labor plays an important role in primary campaigns. This assistance is in the form of direct financial contributions and volunteer manpower. These workers answer 'phones, staff campaign offices, knock on doors, help with mailings, drive voters to the polls on election day, babysit so that voters can get out to the polls, and do research on some of the campaign issues. They also represent a large constituency and are thus able to rally support for those candidates and those issues which are favorable to labor.

> In the Democratic party in Michigan, as far as I'm concerned, it's the Democratic Labor party. And they might as well call it the Labor party, because if you watch them vote on the floor, if labor is for something, they'll all support it and if labor is against it, generally speaking — there are some exceptions — they're all against it.

When the fact that Michigan's major governmental service lies in the field of education is taken into consideration, it is, therefore, not surprising to find that various education interest groups are perceived as being an important lobby in the Michigan state legislature.[4] The state has some ninety colleges and universities, both private and public, within its borders. Here are two responses to a question on lobbies:

> The most powerful lobby group? Well education, of course. They've been eating out of the public trough for years. Most of them work one-hundred-and-eighty days a year . . . That's about one-half of what the average working man works per year. The state picks up all of their retirement and social security, except for the 5% they're paying. We match that with 11%. It's the biggest bill we have every year, . . . twenty-five million dollars a month. So natrually they would have the strongest lobbying group, involving . . . millions of kids, kindergarten through grade 12, and 110,000 school teachers, involving all the community colleges. So they are the most tremendous lobby force in Lansing.

> The MEA and the Michigan Federation of Teachers are the two, the MEA being larger. But when I taught school — I was a former teacher — I belonged to the Federation, and I have a certain kinship with the Federation. In those days, that was the militant group. And now the MEA is a militant group too . . . MEA is somewhat like a semi-public lobby because they're for education. No one's really that much against it.

Another interest group which was mentioned frequently is the Michigan Farm Bureau. One legislator explained the reason for its influence on the Michigan legislature:

> Of course, rurally, the Michigan Farm Bureau is way out in front of all the rural groups, as far as legislative power is concerned. And they have a very definite program. They have lobbyists on the job, legislative committees, legislative seminars, lots of contact with legislators, the Governor's office, and so on . . . They have complete organizations from the community right on to the national level. They have community Farm Bureau discussion groups that meet once a month and have signed material to discuss. Material goes to each individual member and special material to the discussion leader and other local officers. And they have county Farm Bureau resolution committees and legislative committees. They have various area meetings, district meetings, and state conventions, national conventions —

all this and that. All the time the members are kept currently informed on what's going on, and if some real crisis comes up, the folks at the state office call their district men, who are paid men; they call the folks in their district . . . They call this the telephone grid. And inside just a few hours, thousands of people can be alerted to this thing . . . And you can, in a day or two's time, see a total change in atmosphere around here on some issue, for that sort of procedure.

When it was pointed out to several legislators that it seems strange that, in the state which is the home of the automobile industry, the automobile lobby was not perceived at the forefront of pressure groups, the legislators responded that indeed, the automobile industry lobby was very influential, but that the lobby preferred to maintain a low profile. Most legislators who were interviewed knew, by name, the lobbyists which represented the various automotive companies. These lobbyists, however, didn't make their presence felt unless there was a particular piece of legislation under consideration which was of importance to the interests which they represent. One legislator explained:

General Motors has a lobbyist down here — very soft sell. And I've had — in the nine years I've been down here, I've had lunch, I've had a meal with the General Motors loybbist once. Really soft sell; very, very low profile. I think, by the decision of the corporation, they don't want to get charged with hard sell. Chrysler's a little hard sell. And the General Motors lobbyist, when he took me to lunch, he took me out to Michigan Union — out to the College to eat — cafeteria! I couldn't believe it.

Although the automobile industry is the state's leading industry, its lobby is not overly conspicuous in the Michigan legislature. In a study of lobbying by Harmon Zeigler and Michael Baer, the authors were surprised to find that in Oregon, where the lumber industry is among that state's largest income producers, the lumber industry was not ranked among the ten most powerful pressure groups in the state.[5] They suggested the following theory to explain their anomalous finding:

It may be that the economy of the state is so dependent on the lumber industry — that what is good for the lumber industry is so often good for the state too — that legislators usually find themselves in agreement with lumber lobbyists apparently of their own accord without perceptible exercise of power on the part of the lobbyist.[6]

This interpretation might also explain the relationship between the Michigan legislature and the automobile industry lobby. Zeigler and Baer also pointed out that "Business lobbyists are inclined to define their role as one of stopping 'bad bills' rather than pushing for the passage of 'good bills'."[7] The industry, therefore, does not have to rely primarily on pressure as a lobbying technique but rather, can employ a soft sell approach.[8]

The techniques of the interest groups vary. Many of the lobbyists take legislators out to lunch and wine and dine them. Some rely on their testimony before a standing committee which is seeking information on a particular bill. Others will buttonhole a lawmaker in his office. Still others rely on the forcefulness of their arguments. The following excerpts are some of the techniques applied by lobbyists, as described by two legislators:

> The barbers will take you and wine you and dine you and buy you filet mignon. There was a saying down here: "You can eat and drink yes, and vote no."

> Most of them, it's a matter of appearing before a committee, offering testimoney, sending us printed matter, analyzing what they're up to, presenting their arguments, and alerting their people back home as to what's going on and getting pressure from there into here.

By common consent, the vast majority of legislators considered the most effective lobbyist to be one whose word was reliable.

> I think today, with the legislature which is reimbursed adequately, the effective guy, the effective lobbyist is the guy who will present his case fairly and squarely, and openly and honestly. It's the guy who will provide the legislator with information, background materials, and so on, when he's asked to, and who just comes on as a knowledgeable, thoughtful guy. You always know he's representing his interest, but as long as he does it squarely, he's going to be effective up there.

> It's a matter of getting to know that individual representing that group. Is he a man of integrity? Because all you have to do is mislead a legislator one time and word gets around. The only thing you have in politics, really, is your word.

> If a lobbyist deceives a member of the legislature just once, his usefulness is pretty well terminated. So the lobbyist has got to be factual, got to be fair. And if he's asked for information, he's got to supply it and be careful that he knows what he's talking about.

Thus, the most effective lobbyist is one who can be relied upon for honesty and service. Some lobbying techniques are ineffective. Here are some examples:

> Mass mailings and form letters especially aggravate me. And then we get a letter just saying you're opposed, and not giving any reasons.

> It means absolutely nothing to me to be taken out to dinner with my committee members . . . I went to one of those dinners once, that this particular group ran. It's a nice dinner — good food, nice conversation. They didn't go around, they didn't talk shop. But I can just do without that. I've got stuff all the time going on, and I can just do without it.

> Petitions, I don't think, are very potent. Of course, you can get a petition to anything, and a lot of those you don't know how to answer . . . Maybe they've got insufficient addresses, or you don't even know whether those folks are actually your constituents or whether they live some where else,

and you're pretty well sure they didn't know fully what they were saying when they signed . . . I don-t think that is of much consequence. And to get a whole lot of simultaneous letters, all worded the same and typed on the same typewriter and come off of the same mailing lists.

Although the legislators have mixed feelings about some of the techniques employed by the lobbyists, most do not perceive interest groups as a nuisance to be tolerated, but as a positive force which makes real contributions to the legislature. The information which the lobbies provide is considered to be vital. Some legislators claimed, during the interviews, that without interest groups the staff requirements of the legislature would expand enormously. One legislator stated that:

I think that overall, it would be a detriment to the legislative process if there were no lobbyists. There is, simply, not the fund of knowledge in one-hundred-and-ten men and women in the House and thirty-eight in the Senate to adequately cope with all the informational needs that are required to adequately consider legislation. Or, to put it another way, if we are to eliminate lobbying . . . the result would be a need for a fantastically increased staff. We would have to go out and, on our own, through hired staff people, secure the information which today is given freely to the state through those interest groups. And don't forget that many times there are many issues. One interest group will be for it and another interest group will be opposed to it. So you have a value of information from conflicting points of view.

It is fitting, therefore, that lobbyists are viewed in a positive light — for the information and research which they provide free of charge. Most legislators were confident that the information they received from the lobbyists was accurate. The legislators were not concerned that they may be overly dependent upon the lobbies for their information. Some of the older, more senior legislators noted that the Michigan legislature is far less dependent upon lobbyists today to provide information than they were prior to 1964. Some of the abuses that occurred around that time were related by the following legislators:

Years ago, in this legislature, they pretty much called the shots. The Insurance Committee or the insurance lobby would practically name the chairman of the Insurance Committee, name the members. The Farm Bureau, which is a tremendous political power, would practically name who went on Appropriations, who went on Agriculture and Taxation.

There was a time, in the Michigan legislature, when a member was paid three dollars a day for every day the legislature was in session. Now, with that kind of pay scale, believe me — if you wanted to serve up there and you were a man of modest means, you had to have somebody pick up your damned dinner check and your hotel accommodation, or you couldn't afford to go. Unless you wanted to pack a lunch and sleep in your car . . . Not that's gone today . . . The legislators are paid seventeen thousand dollars a year (1972). They're paid reasonable expenses up there, so that there's no need for that kind of thing any more, that open, blatant approach is no longer taken. I haven't heard, in my term up there, one example where a legislator is provided a woman by a lobbyist, but I've heard stories about the old days.

Many of the findings of this paper regarding lobbies and their relationship to the legislators are in conformance with the aforementioned study of lobbying by Zeigler and Baer. Michigan's legislators indicated that organizations representing education and labor interests were among the most prominent of this state's pressure groups. Zeigler and Baer found that in the course of their study, these two groups — that is, education and labor — were perceived as having very powerful legislative lobbies.[9] The authors explained that the education lobby was powerful for three particular reasons, firstly, it has a very large membership; secondly, it puts forth active lobbying efforts; and thirdly, education is regarded as a "sacred cow."[10] As one Michigan legislator explained, since, the MEA is regarded as a semi-public lobby, no-one really opposes it. Labor lobbies in state legislatures also possess large memberships and exert strong lobbying efforts.[11] Furthermore. labor interest groups usually have access to large financial resources.[12]

It is possible, however, that the very activities that make these organizations powerful may, in fact, mitigate their efforts. Because the education and labor lobbies are generally promoting legislation, they are dependent upon persuasive techniques. This could reduce their effectiveness, since "legislators need information but resent pressure and do not like to think of themselves as vulnerable to the persuasive efforts of lobbyists."[13] This corresponds to the legislators' emphasis on the informational aspect of interest groups, rather than stressing the persuasive side of lobbies. In part, this is due to the fact that legislators like to perceive themselves as being impressed by reason and intelligence.

The legislators indicated that they did not regard entertaining as a very effective lobbying technique. However, from the lobbyists' point of view, it is a means whereby channels of communication are kept open. It is rare for business matters to be discussed at these social gatherings, unless the legislators themselves raise such issues.[15] Michigan legislators agreed that social occasions were purely social — unless an issue was brought up by a legislator. The committee hearing is generally a legislator's most important source of information, and the lobbyists tend to flock to the committee rooms as the focal point of their contact with the legislators.[16] Admittedly, the legislators welcome the information they receive from interest groups, especially that which is of a technical nature. Both studies have reflected this fact. As Zeigler and Baer noted, the gathering of information through technical research is one on which state legislators rely heavily since, unlike members of Congress, state legislators usually do not have staff assistance to perform such research.[17]

---

[1] **The Detroit News,** January 21, 1973, p. 4A.

[2] **Ibid.**

[3] William J. Keefe and Morris S. Ogul, **The American Legislative Process: Congress and the States** (Englewood Cliffs, N.J.: Prentice-Hall Inc., 1968), p. 369.

[4] "Michigan", **Encyclopaedia Britannica,** 15th ed., Marcropaedia Vol. XII (1974), 108.

[5] Harmon Zeigler and Michael Baer, **Lobbying: Interaction and Influence in American State Legislatures** (Belmont, California: Wadsworth Publishing Co., inc., 1969), p. 34.

[6] **Ibid.**

[7] **Ibid.,** p. 134.

[8] **Ibid.**

[9] **Ibid.,** p. 194.

[10] **Ibid.,** p. 195.

[11] **Ibid.**

[12] **Ibid.**

[13] **Ibid.,** p. 202.

[14] **Ibid.,** p. 83.

[15] **Ibid.,** p. 191.

[16] **Ibid.,** p. 164.
[17] **Ibid.,** p. 103.

CHAPTER VII

POLICY OUTPUTS OF THE MICHIGAN LEGISLATURE

In general, when considering a legislature it is the lawmaking function which comes to mind. The legislature is viewed in terms of the bills which come before it. There is usually little thought given to the manner in which the members of the legislature arrive at their decisions on whether or not to support the passage of the legislation which comes before them for their attention. In Michigan, over three thousand bills are introduced in the state legislature in any given year. It is impossible, obviously, for a single lawmaker to have complete and first-hand knowledge of all the bills on which he will have to vote yea or nay during the year. One method which is utilized by a legislator to reach his decision is to peruse the analyses which are provided by the various governmental agencies, dealing with the subject matter of each bill. Another factor which helps a legislator in deciding how he will vote on a particular bill is the judgment of one or more of his fellow legislators, in whom he has a great deal of trust and confidence. In his own words, here is one legislator's description of some major factors which he employs to assist himself in arriving at a decision:

> If it is an area that I have no expertise, but I do have an interest and I want to learn, I will study the bill and any analyses of the bill that might be available. For example, tax bills — Treasury will put out . . . an analysis for you . . . However, I don't want to mislead you. There are thousands of bills introduced, hundreds of which are going to end up on the calendar. And many of them are going to be in areas in which you have neither knowledge nor interest. Now, on those kinds of bills, what you generally will do is pick out the guys that you trust who have the knowledge and interest.

One Senator emphasized other sources of information which he relies upon to help him come to a decision in areas where he lacks firsthand knowledge:

> There are a number of ways. One is the analysis of the bill that is put out by the department. Obviously, that's going to be slanted to their position. If They're for it, fine; if they're against, they are going to write their analysis in that way. Interest groups, as you call them, certainly put input into it. Committee meeting hearings that are held, which we attempt to attend as st we can. Talking to citizens in your own community — they'll bring it up to you or they'll call you and talk to you about it. and then, after we put all these things together, we finally reach some general conclusions as to how people feel, why they feel the way they do about the legislation. And you make the decision.

Thus, the sources relied upon to arrive at a decision, apart from one's own judgment, are varied. In addition to those mentioned in the preceding quotations, the list would have to include staff opinions, research carried out by committees, and input from various governmental agencies.

In *The Legislative System*, John Wahlke distinguished between three types of decision makers in a legislature: the trustee, who relies on his own conscience; the delegate, who reflects the advice of his constituents; and the politico, who combines both of these traits.[1] According to Wahlke, most legislators assume the role to trustee.[2] A plurality of the Michigan legislators, by their own admission, concur with Wahlke's finding. When questioned, most legislators responded that they relied on their own knowledge and personal judgment as the principal basis of their decisions. Constituent input was mentioned infrequently in regard to decision making. For this reason, it was not utilized as an individual category in the breakdown of sources of influence. Bryan Jones has provided an explanation for the legislators' apparent independence of the desires and attitudes of their respective constituencies.[3] A legislator who comes from a district considered to be politically safe generally will be representing a homogeneous constituency.[4] He will, therefore, unconsciously reflect the attitudes of his district. In comparison, a legislator who has been elected from a competitive district usually has a heterogeneous constituency.[5] This fact does not make him beholden to those he represents because, firstly, with so varied a constituency it is difficult to know all of the different opinions that are present, and secondly, such a legislator is less reluctant to risk deviation since it is unlikely that, in so doing, he would alienate a majority of his constituents simultaneously.[6] Thus, "no matter whether the legislator was elected from a competitive or a safe district, or whether he adopted a delegate or trustee role orientation, his attitudes are consistently the major guide to his voting decisions."[7]

Besides the legislators' own judgment, their next most important source of influence was the knowledge and judgment of their fellow legislators in whom they had a great deal of trust. Following these sources of information and influence, the legislators then turned to staff, interest groups, and lastly, committees.[8] None of the legislators mentioned debate on the floor of the House or Senate as playing a significant role in their decision making process. When presented with a question pertaining to floor debate, the response of the following legislator was typical of those received:

I think debate changes very few minds. It gives an opportunity for a man to express himself. On amendments it's different. Amendments that are offered to bills are debated. Now, this is new subject matter, again, on what the amendments do, what effect they'd have. And the debate, I think, has an impact, a much stronger effect. But if it's a major piece of legislation, I don't think debate changes many minds on the floor of the Senate.

Even in party caucuses, debate does not seem to play much of a role. One of the Representatives related this somewhat humorous account, which demonstrates the limited impact of debate:

I made an impassioned speech one time, before the Democratic caucus. And afterwards, going up on the elevator, . . . a young liberal from Flint said: "that was really a great speech. You were very articulate."
. . . Of course, the caucus had not gone along with me, and I looked at him and I said: "Yes, but I've learned that the members are not swayed by rhetoric." He said: "No, . . . nor by logic."

It has already been noted that constituent relations occupy a significant portion of a legislator's day. Some of this time is taken up by mail he receives. The legislators were asked about the impact that mail from their constituents has on the decision making process. There appear to be several important factors which are necessary in order for a letter to have an effect. First of all, the letter must indicate that the writer is informed, not simply conveying sentiments or opinions based on ignorance of the facts. Secondly, the letter must be the work of an individual, rather than that of an organized pressure group. Thirdly, the letter must come from a member of the legislator's home district. The quantity of mail expressing a particular view will also have some bearing on the legislaor's decision, as will the legislator's open-mindedness relating to that specific piece of legislation. If a legislator has made up his mind to either support or oppose a bill and is firmly committed to his position, mail will not change his opinion. Some legislators had opinions on this matter which were representative of the responses received regarding a question on the influence of legislators' mail:

I read all the mail we get, and I think it's a reflection of some of the views of the district. I also realize that mail is very special interest and the only people that write it are those who usually have a particular reason about a particular bill. And they're either strongly for or against. The mail that is most effective, as far as I'm concerned, is that which analyzes it — not to say "vote no" or "vote yes" but somebody that says "I think you ought to vote for it because here is what I see it doing." Or "You ought to vote no because I think it would have these detrimental effects." That's an important letter to me, as far as I'm concerned, because it may produce various reasons that I had thought of but sort of said "well, I wonder if that's a really valid reason."

If it's individual letters from my constituents, hand-written, I read them. I'll answer them. I'll listen to them. If it's a form letter from some group or something, I'll throw them in the waste basket.

The lawmakers were also asked how important a role their political party played in the decision making process. Just how much consideration did the legislators give to party policy when they voted on a bill? The overwhelming consensus among the legislators of both houses was that the party plays a rather small role in determining how a legislator will vote on a particular issue. Whether he is a Democrat or a Republican, he has a great deal of latitude in making his decisions. One legislator said this: "I think 95% of the bills are non-partisan in nature, and so you can pretty much make up your own mind as to how you think it affects your constituency." The remainder of the bills are generally those involving controversial social and/or economic matters which will have a considerable impact on the state budget, and are thus of greatest interest to the political parties. These bills are concerned primarily with taxation, appropriations, welfare, education, and the regulation of business and labor. It is these issues, then, which are most likely to separate the legislators along party lines and to evoke a partisan response.[9]

There are certain other matters where a legislator is expected to follow party policy. These would include organizational matters and the drawing of district boundaries. In the area of organization, a party member is expected to vote for his party leadership, e.g., speaker, majority leader, committee chairmen, etc. The same applies when it comes to drawing up district lines. It is expected that a legislator will ". . . vote for the best possible plan that would give the party the best possible chance and the maximum number of districts."

If a party member should fail to support his party in these vital areas, he risks retaliatory action by the party Hierarchy. While such occurrences are rare, there have been some occasions when the party has taken action. One such instance involved a former chairman of the Michigan Senate caucus, Republican Charles Zoller. Zoller favored a Congressional redistricting plan that would reduce the number of safe seats for his party. The Republicans in the Senate voted to remove Zoller from his position as caucus chairman. It was plainly a disciplinary action.[10] There are other ways in which the parties can discipline one of their own members, as this legislator describes:

If he has some legislation that he's interested in, maybe it never moves. Come to committee appointments and you put him on Marine Affairs instead of Appropriations. Comes along election time, and you don't help any; maybe you even help his opponent if you've got some money to distribute, he doesn't get any of it. You don't give him all the staff service that he'd like to have.

Another method of punishing a maverick is the use of redistricting at the earliest opportunity:

> If they don't like somebody, particularly who's crossed them a number of times, they'll do their best every ten years to make it difficult, when the redistricting comes, for them to get elected. It's hard to beat a fellow in an entrenched constituency. But when they get to change those lines, then look out!

On very rare occasions, the party may decide to purge one of its own members from its ranks. One such example, which was mentioned in Chapter IV of this paper, was the case of Richard Friske.[11] This form of drastic action occurs rarely, and is extremely difficult to execute. One legislator had the following explanation for the difficulty in maintaining party discipline:

> We have, in Michigan, what is known as an open primary. Anybody — anybody can run for political office and name their party. . . . This gives rise, in my opinion, to the problem we've faced over the years in our legislature — of a maverick. He's a Republican, but he ran as a Democrat in a relatively conservative, white, homeowners' section of Detroit, for an example. And so you end up with an exceptionally conservative Republican who calls himself a Democrat. And he's got a good name and he keeps getting re-elected by the people of his district. How do you cope with him? How do you discipline him?

To reiterate, most legislators rely primarily upon their own personal judgment to arrive at their decisions as to how they will vote on legislation. Next in importance is the opinion of other legislators whose advice and expertise they respect and trust. Thirdly, the composition and opinions of each legislator's constituency will have some bearing on how he votes. These three factors are essentially the basis for legislative decision making. The legislators, for the most part, have a good deal of independence in their relationships with their political parties.

The next area that was examined, together with some of the members of the legislature, was conflict in the assembly and the major sources of this conflict. According to most of the legislators who were either interviewed and/or returned questionnaires, the major conflict in the Michigan state legislature did not occur, as might be supposed, according to partisan divisions but rather, along liberal versus conservative allegiances. In other words, when important bills come up for consideration, the legislature breaks most often along liberal and conservative ideologies. "Virtually all issues have some sort of an idelogical flavor. Therefore, in the legislature, I would say the liberal/conservative conflict is the evident one." The legislators ranked regional conflicts as the second most important area of dissension, particularly friction between the cities and the rural areas. The third most important source of conflict was said to be that between the cities and the suburbs, followed by Detroit versus the remainder of the state. These categories are not entirely separate and often overlap. One legislator described the legislative conflicts as he perceived them:

> To me, it's not a question of city versus rural, or city versus suburban. You have to throw all three in, and that's extremely important. There are some issues where you can get city and suburb — particularly in south-eastern Michigan — on the one side and rural on the other. You might get it for mass transit . . . However, you get into something like open housing and you'll get a strange alliance of the city — in this case, it might be the city of Detroit — and the boondocks against the suburbs. Now, the reason is that a lot of Republicans in outstate Michigan don't feel threatened by open housing, for instance. What the hell do they care? My district is 99.7% white. I don't have any blacks. I don't have any minorities in my district. So why the hell should I care? . . . So you get an alliance. Very often it's very dramatic . . . But it shifts. And the suburbs are the swingers. They can swing the rural, or they can swing the city, or they can be for themsleves. And so that is a genuine confrontation between differences of opinion. They play a very important role. And they became more important, as the years have gone on, because of one man-one vote. I mean, with that decision, really, the suburbs' power, I think, would probably increase far more than really the city or the rural areas. Now, the rural areas are, if anything, well, they're not decreasing but they're barely holding their own. In some parts, they are decreasing. And of course, Detroit lost 150,000 people between 1960 and 1970. And those people are moving out into the suburbs. So these people are — they're becoming very, very important and they really make or break a lot of issues.

There were some legislators, however, who perceived the rural areas as the swing districts. But all agreed that regional conflicts played an important part in the composition and passage of bills in the legislature. Another legislator expressed his views on the conflicts thusly:

> Well, there is a growing suburban versus inner city conflict. It was, I think, lacking or at least much more minimal some years back. The traditional conflict was city versus rural. In those instances, the rural areas usually won, because we had a mal-apportioned legislature. The one man-one vote principle is not really mitigated in favor of the cities, because what it has done is give rise to a tremendous increase in representation in suburban areas, at the same time that they've been experiencing all the growth. And much of the growth is due to fleeing whites out of the city areas. So that this growing confrontation that I see developing is between the city groups, who are steadily losing strength — they're losing five House seats out of twenty-five this year [1972] with redistricting. Those five seats are being spread among the suburban areas. So we're gaining five, and more and more of the representation from suburbia comes up here just violently anti-city. . . . So that I see it as a tremendously important conflict, with the rural people in the position of being the swing votes — sort of occupying the position that the suburban legislators used to represent. . . . Now the suburban groups have probably got the largest single bloc of votes up there, and how they use that power is going to be damned important in terms of the future.

Implicit in the above statement, although never expressed openly, is the concept of covert racial conflict. The proportion of blacks in the city of Detroit is increasing. By 1970, the population of Detroit was 45% black.[12] Today, it is estimated that Detroit is 50% black. Coleman Young was elected as Detroit's first black mayor in the 1973 elections. It has already been noted that Detroit's white population has been fleeing to the suburbs, thus underlying a supposedly regional conflict that might very well be a racial one.

Yet the impression left after the conclusion of all the interviews and following the analysis of the questionnaires reinforced the belief that ideology was the single most important conflict in the legislature. The regional friction and, following that in importance, partisan conflicts appear to play a relatively minor role in Michigan's assembly. In the words of one legislator:

> First of all, 90% of all the bills that go through here have no partisan connotations. You have some Democrats voting for it and some Democrats voting against it. You have some Republicans for it and some against it. You have to boil it down to each individual issue. I would say that 80% of the organizations will support the legislation that goes through here. When you get into revenue sharing, you do have the battle between cities versus rural or suburban schools and . . . there's a little friction there.

Another source of conflict in Michigan's legislature is the dissension that arises between the legislative and the executive brances of the state assembly. On the whole, the legislators had good self-images, irrespective of the party affiliation, and staunchly defended the Michigan legislature as an institution. All were proud of the work they had accoplished. Most, however, expressed some concern regarding the image of the legislators and their work that was conveyed in the press. They felt that, in comparison to the favorable treatment customarily received by the executive branch of Michian's government, the legislative branch was treated unfairly. The legislators expressed a certain wariness and some jealousy of the executive branch, and there was considerable concern about the executive encroaching upon the powers of the legislature. The following quotations are taken from some of the interviews with the legislators, and express their sentiments regarding the friction between the two branches of government and their feelings about their own legislature:

> Michigan is a large state, with a large population and a very diverse economy. And it has demanded continuing increases in legislative attention. So I think that the salaries that are offered in Michigan have attracted — increasingly attracted — better men to the legislature and enabled them, once there, to act independently and not be dependent on special interests to subsidize their stay in Lansing. I think that

procedurally — our legislative procedures, the committee system we use, the way we get bills through from introduction to final enrolling — is above average. So that we move an awful lot of legislation. We move it relatively expeditiously. . . . . So I'd have to say that our unique feature is, we are probably one of the better legislatures in the country.

I think, in my judgment, that the Michigan legislature is probably one of the most honorable bodies that I've had the pleasure of working with. That doesn't mean that I agree with it all the time. I think the treatment and deliberation that goes into the passage of legislation here, almost without exception, I think is very good for the effects of the state.

I think Michigan has probably one of the most responsive and progressive legislatures . . . not because I'm a member, but because of past surveys that indicated Michigan ranks very high in its capacity, in its work habits, its rules, its organizational structure. I think Michigan has been very progressive — in the last ten years particularly.[13]

Now that I'm in the legislature, I've gotten more and more strongly attached to the legislature as an institution, even while I find so many things that are unsatisfactory and disappointing. Even while I may not like many of the individuals in the legislature, and cringe at some of the people that are in the legislature, perhaps that gives it the kind of reputation that I think it has. Still in all, I keep building and building this kind of, this feeling of affection and defensiveness for the legislative branch of government.

Several of the legislators who were interviewed had served in the Michigan assembly for the previous ten years, and a few had been there even longer. These men made constant mention of the improvements they had witnessed in the state legislature since 1964. Most believed that the legislature has become more innovative and professional in recent years. A comparison of the legislation that was passed in the 1961-1962 period with that of the 1971-1972 legislative session is enlightening.

Specifically, by the time the 1962 legislative session drew to a close, the important legislation that had been passed included various nuisance taxes, improvement in school financing, bills concerned with health and mental hygiene, and the approval of a State Fair Authority.[14]

The year 1962 was an important election year in Michigan. The Governor's office was being challenged and the members of the state House of Representatives were also being elected that same year. The salient issues in Michigan at the time were unemployment and the adoption of a new state constitution. George Romney, the Republican candidate for Governor, advocated adopting the new constitution. Romney had helped to initiate the move for a new constitution and had been important in influencing the shape of the proposed document.

His support, then, was no surprise. Romney emphasized his success as the president of American Motors Corporation in promoting his capacity to run a financially sound state government.[15] In 1961, under Democratic Governor John Swainson, Michigan had a budget deficit of eighty-five million dollars. Swainson suggested the installation of a new state income tax to help offset future budget deficits, but this idea had little public support and did not help his cause.[16] By late September, 1962, public opinion polls indicated that a large number of disenchanted Democrats were switching to Romney.[17] Governor Swainson was blamed for the dearth of legislation passed by the assembly that session. Many believed that a Republican Governor would be more effective in dealing with a Republican legislature, which Michigan had in 1962. Furthermore, it would have been difficult to alter the composition of the legislature to any great degree. The Democrats had controlled the Governor's office for fourteen years, and many felt that it was time for a change. The 1962 election attracted the largest non-Presidential vote in Michigan's history. Romney defeated Swainson handily for Governor. Wayne County, which includes the city of Detroit and which was and is traditionally Democratic, accorded Romney 40% of its total vote. Outstate counties also voted heavily for Romney. Swainson had needed 70% of Wayne County's vote to offset Republican support in the remainder of the state.[18] At the same time, the House of Representatives retained its Republican majority.

Ten years later, Michigan was being influenced by national politics. Michigan was holding its first presidential primary in almost fifty years. This had the effect of making certain national issues particularly important in Michigan. Specifically, busing, abortion reform, and the rising crime rate — all important issues in Michigan as well as the rest of the nation — were given a great deal of attention in the state because of their national ramifications. In 1972, the Governor was not up for re-election but both the state Senate and House of Representatives memberships were being challenged. Economically in Michigan, automobile sales were at a record high level and unemployment was low. Consequently, the economy was not a political issues, as it had been in the 1962 elections.

The 1972 November ballot was an especially lengthy and complex one. In addition to the list of elective offices and the candidates seeking to fill them, the ballot contained several propositions. Among these were three of particular significance. The proposal for the institution of a statewide graduated income tax was strongly supported by Governor Milliken and by the Michigan Education Association. It was hoped that this new tax would provide additional monies for educational funding. At the same time, another proposal on the ballot was intended to alleviate the burden of property owners to fund the schools primarily through local property taxes. This proposal would have had the state assume the responsibility for financing the public schools on a statewide equalized basis. The third important proposition was intended to make abortion an individual matter to be decided between a woman and her physician.

The length and complexity of the ballot may have contributed to the defeat of these propositions. Despite Nixon's nationwide landslide victory in the 1972 presidential election, his majority in Michigan was limited to 57% of the votes. Still, this was the first time since 1956 that Michigan voters had supported a Republican presidential candidate. Nixon's victory did not have a "coattail effect" in the state legislature. In the Senate, the Democrats retained their nineteen to nineteen split and in the House of Representatives, the Democrats increased their majority.

In comparing the legislation that resulted from the 1972 session with that from the 1962 legislature, there are notable variances. In 1972, the Michigan legislature approved a bill that would provide funding for mass transit, approved a presidential primary for the state, passed a no-fault automobile insurance bill, ratified legislation to permit a state lottery and bingo games, expanded bonding for housing, increased aid for environmental protection — a measure designed to protect the state's lakes and streams, passed a landlord/tenant security deposit agreement, strengthened roadside billboard regulations, and approved a new formula to handle tax and revenue sharing.[19] The 1962 legislative session consisted of 104 session days. During this time, 1,223 bills were introduced in the legislature and of these, 243 were enacted.[20] In comparison, there were 120 days in the 1972 legislative session. In this period, 3,914 pieces of legislation were introduced, of which 621 actually became law.[21] Clearly, then, the number and character of innovative and imaginative programs passed by the 1972 legislature were far superior to the legislation approved ten years previously.

Another example which illustrates the differences between the 1962 and 1972 legislative sessions is general state expenditures. In 1962, the Michigan state legislature allocated a total of $1,565,183,000 for various programs.[22] The largest amount of money — 37% of the total — was spent on public education, highways received 27%, another 11% went toward public welfare programs, 7.5% was spent on health care, and natural resources received 2% of the allocation.[23] Ten years later, the 1972 legislature had increased the state's expenditure to $4,531,982,000 for that year.[24] Education had grown to 40% of the total amount, public welfare now consumed 23%, highway expenditure had decreased to 12% of the available funds, 7% was spent on health care, and natural resources again received 2% of the total allocation.[25] The following table shows the total amounts, in thousands of dollars, designated for six major areas during these two periods:

TABLE 5
A COMPARISON OF STATE EXPENDITURES*

Category	1962	1972
Education	582,769	1,831,774
Highways	433,855	597,557
Public Welfare...............	167,140	1,025,237
Hospitals.....................	100,161	231,622
Natural Resources	32,084	84,053
Health	17,863	102,542

* Statistics are taken from: The Council of State Governments, *The Book of the States, 1964-1965* (Lexington, Kentucky, 1965), Table 5, p. 208 and the 1974-1975 edition of the same publication, Table 5, p. 210.

There are several factors which help to explain the considerable increase in Michigan's total expenditure ten years after the 1962 budget. Inflation had risen by 34.7% in this period, accounting for part of the overall increase. According to Ira Sharkansky, incrementalism has a strong influence on state budgets.[26] However, on examining the data in *Table 5*, it is evident that the increased expenditures in 1972 are excessive of the total that would have resulted had inflation and incrementalism been the only factors. After investigation, it would seem that legislative reapportionment is primarily responsible for the large increase in the total 1972 expenditure and the re-allocation of state funds. "The distribution of state expenditures is significantly influenced by legislative apportionment. The longer a state's experience with reapportionment, the greater its propensity to spend in favor or urban needs."[27] These needs would include welfare, education, health, and hospitals. Spending for highways and natural resources is mostly a product of the absence of urbanization and industrialization.[28] Thus, the decrease in highway expenditures from 27% of the total budget in 1962 to 12% in 1972 is indication of the growth of Michigan's urban centers and the decline of rural representation during this period. The

95

simultaneous increase in the allotment of 11% of the state's funds in 1962 to 23% ten years later for public welfare programs supports the contention the "reapportionment will result in changes of fiscal decisions in the direction of urban interests."[29] The greatest increase in expenditures occurred in the years between 1966 and 1969, in the fields of higher education, local schools, public welfare, highways, and hospitals — illustrating a relationship between legislative reapportionment and changes in the state's public policy.[30] The reapportionment of the Michigan legislature in 1964 contributed significantly to the increased spending of state funds in those areas mentioned above. The total expenditure continues to grow each year, both in dollars spent and in the increased percentages of the total which are utilized for urban programs, although the rate of growth has slowed since 1969.

Despite some rather impressive and innovative legislation, the members of Michigan's state legislature perceived their assembly to have a poor press image. This view was particularly true in relation to the good press attributed to the Governor. The legislators themselves had few solutions to offer in order to solve this problem. Some believed that a seminar for the newsmen might be beneficial to their cause. It was felt that many reporters were ignorant of the legislative process and the work of the members of the assembly. Others thought that perhaps more direct communication with their constituents, either through mailings or via district offices, would aid their cause. The following remarks are some of the legislators' comments concerning what they perceived to be their poor image in Michigan newspapers:

> The thing that bothers me more than anything is credibility with the people. I don't know how we achieve that, how we work it with the press. Because by nature, the legislature is the whipping boy. This is just the nature of a democracy. The same as the Congress of the United States is the whipping boy. I would hope there is some way we could develop a relationship with the press and with the constituents, so that we could keep the people informed of what we're doing and what we're attempting to do. I hate to think that every legislator has to become a newsman and be sending news bulletins all over the state. But sometimes it's just tremendously difficult to get a message out to your people unless you do that. I don't know.

Yet another theory is expressed by this legislator:

> I suspect that it's because of jealousies — individual animosities between legislators and the press. The fact that the executive is not in a fishbowl, so to speak, as we are daily — constantly before the public, in public meetings. Much of what goes on in the executive office is never open to the public, or at least the public never observes it. Nor does the reporter . . . When a legislator takes a trip, the study committee is called a junket. When the Governor goes to the governors' conference in Arizona, it's not called a junket . . . If you take each individual legislator, you'll find that most of them are intelligent, honest, concerned people — just like the man back home who is concerned about government. It's just a few who make it bad for everyone.

[1] John C. Wahlke **et al.**, **The Legislative System** (New York: John Wiley and Sons, Inc., 1962), p. 286.

[2] **Ibid.**

[3] Bryan D. Jones, "Competitiveness, Role Orientations and Legislative Responsiveness," **Journal of Politics,** XXXV (November, 2973), 924-947.

[4] **Ibid.,** p. 935..

[5] **Ibid.**, p. 935.

[6] **Ibid.**

[7] Ibid., p. 945.

[8] Of eighteen legislators interviewed, here is a breakdown of the sources they relied upon the most to reach their decisions:

1) Self	48.50%		4) Interest Groups	8.43%	
2) Other Members	20.50%		5) Committees	7.32%	
3) Staff	8.75%		6) Other	6.50%	
		TOTAL: 100%			

[9] Thomas R. Dye, "State Legislative Politics," **Politics in the American States,** ed. Herbert Jacob and Kenneth Vines (Boston: Little, Brown and Co., 1965), p. 188.

[10] Gongwers News Service, **Michigan Report,** XI, No. 99 (May 19, 1972), p. 1.

[11] The successful purge of Richard Friske is discussed in Chapter IV, **The Legislators,** on pages 87-88.

[12] **1970 Census of Population.** U.S. Department of Commerce, Bureau of the Census, p. 24-56.

[13] The Citizens Conference on State Legislatures, State Legislatures: **An Evaluation of Their Effectiveness** (New York: Praeger Publishers, 1971), p. 40. This source, which has been previously cited, has ranked Michigan's legislature as eighth in the nation and corroborates this legislator's statement.

[14] Gongwers New Service, **Michigan Report,** I, No. 108 (June 28, 1962), p. 2.

[15] **The Detroit Free Press,** September 4, 1962, p. 1.

[16] **The Detroit Free Press,** September 23, 1962, p. 1.

[17] **Ibid.**

[18] **The Detroit Free Press,** November 7, 1962, p. 1.

[19] Gongwers News Service, **op. cit.,** XI, (December 29, 1972), pp. 1-13.

[20] The Council of State Governments, **The Book of the States, 1964-1965** (Lexington, Kentucky, 1965), p. 60.

[21] **Ibid.,** 1974-1975, p. 69.

[22] **Ibid.,** 1964-1965, Table 5, p. 208.

[23] **Ibid.**

[24] **Ibid.,** 1974-1975, Table 5, p. 210.

[25] **Ibid.**

[26] Ira Sharkansky, **Spending in the American States** (Chicago: Rand McNally and Co., 1968), p. 18.

[27] H. George Frederickson and Yong Hyo Cho, "Legislative Apportionment and Fiscal Policy in the American States," **Western Political Quarterly, XXVII (March,1974), 35.**

[29] Frederickson and Cho, **op. cit.**

[30] Roger C. Hanson and Robert Crew, Jr., "The Policy Impact of Reapportionment." **Law and Society Review,** VIII (Fall, 1973), 90.

CHAPTER VIII

CONCLUSIONS

This descriptive account of the Michigan State legislature has concerned itself, specifically, with a study of the following, previously mentioned categories: political culture, legislative structure and organization, the legislators, the committee system, legislative leadership, Michigan's political parties, interest groups, and policy outputs. The purpose of this examination of the Michigan legislature is to test the veracity or fallacy of the four primary hypotheses, and of those which are consequently inferred. With this in mind, let us proceed to scrutinize the material which has been presented.

In the introduction to this book, the first hypothesis states:

(1) The typical state legislator is male, white, Protestant, of Anglo-Saxon descent, and has the predominant profession of either lawyer, businessman, or farmer.

The information gathered for the preparation of this study supports this contention — with one noteworthy exception. Farming is no longer among the three main professions of Michigan's legislators. Teaching has replaced farming, as the state's rural representation has been reapportioned according to the rural population. This is a major change from the Michigan legislature in the early 1960's, and from other state legislatures as well. Presently in Michigan, the backgrounds of the legislators are, according to their predominance: law, teaching, and business. Concerning the remainder of this hypothesis, out of 148 legislators in the 1972 Michigan assembly, there were only two female members of the House of Representatives and none in the Senate. Black legislators occupied thirteen of 110 seats in the House and two out of thirty-eight seats in the state Senate. In 1972, about two-thirds of Michigan's legislators were of the Protestant religion. These facts correspond to the assertions stated in the first hypothesis.

Some additional information of significance surfaced during the course of this study. The level of education of a Michigan legislator exceeds that of the population as a whole. Since reapportionment, Michigan law-makers have been younger — averaging just over forty-nine years of age in 1972, as compared to fifty-four years of age in 1962. The salaries of the legislators have also been increased considerably in recent years, as the following table illustrates:

TABLE 6

MICHIGAN LEGISLATIVE SALARIESa

Yearsb	Annual Salary
1949-1952	$ 2,400 + $1,000 for expenses
1953-1954	$ 2,900 + $1,000 for expenses
1955-1960	$ 4,000 + $1,000 for expenses
1961-1962	$ 5,000 + $1,250 for expenses
1963-1964	$ 7,000 + $1,250 for expenses
1965-1966	$10,000 + $2,500 for expenses
1967-1968	$12,500 + $2,500 for expenses
1969-1970	$15,000 + $3,000 for expenses
1971-1974	$17,000 + $2,750 for expenses
1975-1976	$19,000 + $3,300 for expenses

a Source: *Michigan Manual,* biennial editions from 1949 to 1975.

b Prior to 1949, the legislators received three dollars per session day.

The second hypothesis to be evaluated concerns the legislators' introduction to politics and political office, political parties, and interest groups. It asserts that:

(1) Both political parties and interest groups play a significant role in the recruitment of legislative candidates and in the decision-making process in the legislature. Thus:

    a. Both major political parties manifest a strong organization. The strength of party organization may be determined by the perceptions of the legislators themselves, by the regularity of party caucuses in the legislature, or by partisan cohesion on important pieces of legislation, or by all of the above.

    b. These parties have definite and distinct ideologies based upon the traditional liberal/conservative philosophies.

    c. The major interest groups in the legislature are the automotive industry and labor.

Through personal interviews and the use of questionnaires, the legislators indicated that their interest in politics had evolved during their childhood and/or adolescence, and that their decision to seek elective office was made irrespective of their political parties. Very few

100

legislators noted that the party had actively recruited them for a position. None made mention of any interest group in connection with legislative recruitment. For some legislators, a particular event occurred — such as concern over the deterioration of a neighborhood or a moral or civil rights issue — which propelled them into the political arena. The majority of legislators indicated that their prime motivating force was their enjoyment of politics, with its various aspects — the satisfaction that comes from public service, the ability to reform or change things that are inadequate or objectionable, and the excitement that comes with being politically active. Before an individual can enter politics and run for political office, he must have financial backing. In their first campaign for membership in the state legislature, most of the legislators raised their own money and formed their own personal organizations. The legislators also noted that before they sought office, they had to believe that they would be successful, that they had a good chance to win the political positions they were seeking. For this reason, most of the legislators ran in their districts when they did not have to oppose an incumbent. To reiterate, a large consenus of legislators indicated that the party played no role whatsoever in their recruitment for the office of either state Senator or state Representative. Nor did the party participate in the legislators' initial primary campaigns. In regard to the general election, the legislators might receive some financial or volunteer assistance from the party — depending upon the availability or desirability of party support. The legislators run essentially with the help of their own personal organizations and staffs. Thus, when a Michigan legislator joins the state assembly for the first time, he generally enters as an independent agent, beholden neither to his party nor to a particular interest group. Most legislators consider themselves to be self-starters. When the legislators were asked to enumerate those factors which assisted them in their decision making, interest groups were mentioned infrequently. On those occasions when the legislators did consult interest groups, the reason given was the ability of these groups to provide information on particular legislation that was of interest to the legislators. Political parties were not mentioned at all in regard to legislative decision making. The legislators rely primarily upon their own judgment and information. Second to themselves, the recommendation of a fellow legislator in whom a legislator had particular trust and respect would have some degree of influence upon his decision. To further elaborate, floor debate plays an insignificant role in decision making. Legislators consider their mail somewhat, but there are a number of factors which must exist before constituent correspondence will have any bearing on the legislators' decisions.

The primary assertion of this second hypothesis appears to be fallacious. There is no evidence to dispute the legislators' contentions that neither political parties nor interest groups play a significant role in the recruitment of legislative candidates. Those responding to the questionnaires and submitting to personal interviews further asserted that their decision making was independent of party and pressure group influence. There are, however, factors other than the legislators' own responses which temper this aspect of the hypothesis but do not totally negate its validity. If Zeigler's and Baer's premise that legislators like to think of themselves as being "impressed by reason and intelligence" is accepted, then these individuals would be understandably reluctant to admit that either political parties or interest groups unduly influence their decisions.[1] In addition, while the legislators noted that most of the legislation that comes before the Michigan assembly is not of a partisan nature, the proportionately small number of bills concerned with issues involving taxation, appropriations, welfare, and the regulation of business and labor have a very significant impact on the state's economy and tend to evoke a partisan response from the legislative membership. It is in these areas where the legislators display a strong degree of party cohesion.[2] Furthermore, since the legislators identify with either the Democratic or the Republican party, it is logical to assume that they are in agreement with their chosen party's basic ideology. Thus it is likely that a legislator will reflect his party's philosophy in his decision making, without the party exerting overt pressure.

When the subject of political parties was discussed with the legislators, they made a distinction between the state party organizations and the party organizations within the legislature itself. Contrary to expectation, both parties appear to have loose, rather weak organizations at the state level. This conclusion is based upon several factors. Because the parties did not participate actively in the recruitment and the campaigns of most of the legislators, they personally perceived their state party organizations as ineffective and decentralized. The strength and health of the party organizations varies from county to county. Generally, however, the state party organizations of both the Democrats and the Republicans are ineffectual.

Within the legislature itself, party strength is more visible. Both the Democratic party and the Republican party caucus at least once a month. Party members vote cohesively regarding redistricting, organizational matters, such as the election of committee chairmen and the composition of committees, and particularly concerning the election of their officers, for example, the Speaker of the House.

The legislators had definite views concerning party ideology — both that of their own party and of the opposing party as well. The difference between the Democratic party and the Republican party is most visible in regard to economic issues. From the legislators' perspective, the Democratic party is more willing to spend money on various government programs, to employ the powers of government for the purpose of reform, and represents the interests of organized labor and the minority groups. The Republican party, on the other hand, is more cautious when it comes to financing social programs. Republicans emphasize local control of government agencies — decentralization. They stress the need for a balanced budget and, in general, encourage the maintenance of the status quo. Further, Republicans are more representative of business interests.

The Democratic and Republican parties differ in their demographic compositions, as well as in their economic philosophies. In the Michigan state legislature, all of the black legislators and the female members of the assembly are affiliated with the Democratic party. Within the legislature, the Democrats have the largest percentage of minorities — ethnic, racial, and religious. The Republican party is more homogeneous, more representative of white, Anglo-Saxon, Protestant Americans. This aspect of the second major hypothesis is thus supported. The political parties within the legislature are separated from each other by their ideological philosophies which, as evidenced, are based upon traditional liberal/conservative beliefs. The cohesive force of the legislative parties is primarily ideological.

The foregoing discussion of political parties raises the issues of accountability and responsible party government within the Michigan legislature. The state party organizations are, from all indications and as stated previously, weak, loose, and disorderly coalitions. They are heavily decentralized, and lacking in unity and discipline. However, the parties do have some significance. On traditional economic issues, Michigan's political parties offer separate policy alternatives. The parties also represent different socio-economic constituencies and distinct geographical areas. Furthermore, the legislators are identified with their respective parties and the parties' labels generally hold meaning for the legislators, as well as for their constituents.

Evron Kirkpatrick has said: "Party government clearly has instrumental, not intrinsic, value. It was (and is) desired because of the belief that it would enhance the responsibility of the governors to the governed."[3] Dr. Kirkpatrick was a member of The American Political Science Association's Committee on Political Parties from 1946 until

1950 and later took issue with a particular report published by the Committee.[4] This report was criticized, in part, for not taking into account various factors other than political parties that provide accountability and responsibility. To quote:

> Not considered were the possibilities that, in a far-flung heterogeneous nation, decisions might best be made through continued aggregation of interests in the legislature; that, in a heterogeneous nation with multiple issues in every election, it might make more sense to hold individuals rather than parties responsible; that individual accountability to voters might make for better representation of the district; that loose parties might be the only institutions consistent with diffuse decision making, itself a protection against error and tyranny; and that Americans might generally prefer to risk the delays of diffuse decision making than the mistakes of easily mobilized majoritarianism.[5]

Even at the state level, accountability and responsibility can be achieved by means other than and in addition to political parties.

The last aspect of this hypothesis concerns interest groups. The legislators viewed the various interest groups affecting the legislature in a generally favorable light. The major lobbies play some role in the legislators' decision making process. They were considered to be valuable sources of information, believed by most legislators to be accurate. The legislators did not perceive themselves as dependent upon the interest groups for their information but rather, as pleased to have this added source of knowledge at their disposal.

The observations of the legislators, with respect to the principal interest groups in the Michigan legislature, were somewhat surprising. While the expectation that labor was a major interest group in the legislature was substantiated — in particular, regarding the American Federation of Labor (AF of L), and the United Automobile Workers (UAW) — this was not the case regarding the automotive industry. The legislators did not perceive the auto industry as either a major source of influence in the legislative assembly or as a particularly visible interest group. Instead, the Michigan Education Association (MEA), and the American Federation of Teachers (AFT) — the education lobbies — were viewed as being among the principal interest groups. The American Farm Bureau is also an important pressure group in the Michigan legislature, according to the legislators.

The third hypothesis begins by stating that:
(3) There is a high rate of turnover in the Michigan legislature.

In fact, the rate of turnover has declined in the Michigan legislature over the past fifty years. Ray's study on membership stability provides statistics in support of this statement.[6] Ray employed three criteria to ascertain stability: the number of first term legislators, the percentage of legislators seeking re-election, and the average prior service of each member.[7] He found that in Michigan, 74.5% of the total legislative membership was serving its first term of office in 1893.[8] By 1969, this figure had declined to 24%.[9] In regard to career commitment, 31.5% of the members of both houses sought re-election in 1893, whereas by 1965, this number had gradually increased to 92%.[10] In 1893, the average Michigan legislator had .25 years of prior legislative service but by 1969, the legislators averaged two years of previous experience in the state legislature.[11] Although these figures demonstrate an increase in the stability of the Michigan state legislature, the rate of turnover is still about twice that of Congress.[12]

According to the research conducted for this dissertation, seniority can be achieved after only about three successive terms of office. This brings us to the first of the three inferred consequences of the general hypothesis:

a. Factors besides seniority play an important role in the selection of committee chairmen.

While seniority is a factor in attaining a chairmanship position, it does not appear to be an essential element. In the House of Representatives, seniority can be earned after serving three or four two-year terms. In the 1971-1972 Michigan Senate, the thirty-eight Senators were evenly divided in their party affiliation. Because there are about as many majority party members as there are committees in the upper chamber, practically all majority party Senators are able to chair some committee. The most important factors in the selection of committee chairmen are: the experience of an individual in the committee's particular field of jurisdiction, the competence of the legislator, party loyalty, and the ability to get along with one's colleagues. Thus, this aspect of the hypothesis is supported by the evidence provided in this paper.

The next assertion states that:

b. Most of the important legislative assignments are carried out by only a few legislators.

This hypothesis was also borne out by the research. Those legislators holding positions of power also have the responsibility of performing most of the legislative duties. One reason for this is the large staff assigned to an individual of particular importance. Such positions would include the Speaker of the House, the majority and minority leaders in both houses, and the chairmen of important committees. This is particularly true of the Appropriations Committee chairmen in both chambers, and would also include the members of these most important committees in both the House and Senate. The Appropriations Committees are each provided with staff assistance to help the members with their workload. All of the important legislation must be considered by the Appropriations Committees. This guarantees that just over a dozen Representatives in the House, and even fewer members of the Senate, carry out the most important legislative duties. Consequently, out of a total of one hundred and forty-eight legislators, a relative few are responsible for most of the important legislative assignments.

The next hypothesis concerns legislative expertise and asserts that:
c. The Michigan legislature has difficulty in attaining a high degree of expertise.

The Michigan legislators expressed confidence in their ability to acquire knowledge and to be informed regarding the bills they receive for consideration. Most of the legislators had respect for the expertise of their colleagues. The fact that the Senate comes up for re-election every four years provides the members with sufficient time to develop their skill. Many Senators and Representatives arrive at the legislature with knowledge and experience in areas that are beneficial to them in the committees on which they serve. Because the rate of turnover has declined in the last half-century, there are fewer first term legislators that there were fifty years ago, and thus, the legislature is, in general, more experienced. The increase in staff assistance has increased the legislators' ability to cope with complex issues. The input from interest groups and public hearings also contributes to the development of legislative expertise.

While determining legislative expertise on the basis of the legislators' perceptions is a subjective proposition, it is significant that, with very few exceptions, those members of Michigan's legislature who were interviewed perceived their colleagues to be knowledgeable and of a high calibre. The legislators did not indicate any feelings of frustration or inadequacy in grappling with the problems and bills which they regularly confront. The pride and assurance which the members of the legislature expressed for their own performance of their duty, as well as that of their fellow legislators, would indicate that this hypothesis is in error. The legislators are able to acquire their expertise without particular difficulty and within the course of performing their legislative functions.

The concluding hypothesis relates to the oversight function in the legislature:

(4) Finally, although the Michigan legislators are well-staffed in comparison with other states, the legislative branch has a difficult time overseeing the executive agencies and, in fact, does not provide an effective check on the executive branch of Michigan's government.

The overall indication is that the legislative committees do not serve this function. Some of the legislators expressed feelings of frustration in this regard. It was felt that there were too many executive agencies for the legislative committees to be able to maintain any degree of effective control. For the most part, the legislators rely on the auditor-general and on constituent correspondence to inform them of any inefficiency or problem with the executive branch of the state's government. Many legislators admitted that they were not acquainted with the term "oversight function" nor were they aware that this particular function was the responsibility of their committees. This final hypothesis, then, is substantiated and its verification brings this study to its conclusion.

---

[1] Harmon Zeigler and Michael Bar, **Lobbying: Interaction and Influence in American State Legislatures** (Belmont, California: Wadsworth Publishing Co., Inc., 1969), p. 83.

[2] Thomas R. Dye, **Politics in States and Communities** (Englewood Cliffs, N.J.: Prentice-Hall, Inc. 1973), p. 149.

[3] Evron M. Kirkpatrick, "Toward a More Responsible Two-Party System: Political Science, Policy Science, or Pseudo-Science?" **The American Political Science Review**, LXV (December, 1971), 978.

[4] "Toward a More Responsible Two-Party System: A Report of the Committee on Political Parties, American Political Science Association." **The American Political Science Review** (Supplement: Vol. 44, September 1950, No. 3, Part 2).

[5] Kirkpatrick, **op. cit.,** p. 979.

[6] David Ray, "Membership Stability in Three State Legislatures, 1893-1969," **The American Political Science Review,** LXVIII (March, 1974), 106-112.

[7] **Ibid.,** p. 107.

[8] **Ibid.,** p. 108.

[9] **Ibid.**

[10] **Ibid.,** p. 109

[11] **Ibid.,** p. 110.

[12] Kenneth T. Palmer, **State Politics in the United States** (New York: St. Martin's Press, 1972), p. 66.

APPENDIX A

PERSONAL INTERVIEWS

Name	Chamber	Party	Residence
Ballenger, William S., III.	Senate	R	Ovid
Bowman, John T.	Senate	D	Roseville
Cooper, Daniel S.	Senate	D	Oak Park
Dively, Michael A.	House	R	Traverse City
Huffman, Bill S.	House	D	Madison Heights
Kildee, Dale E.	House	D	Flint
Mastin, Philip O., Jr.	House	D	Hazel Park
McCollough, Lucille H.	House	D	Dearborn
Mittan, Ray C.	House	R	Benton Harbor
Powell, Stanley M.	House	R	Ionia
Smart, Clifford H.	House	R	Walled Lake
Spencer, Roy L.	House	R	Attica
Stamm, Anthony	Senate	R	Kalamazoo
Vaughn, Jackie, III.	House	D	Detroit
Zaagman, Milton	Senate	R	Grand Rapids

APPENDIX B

RESPONDENTS TO QUESTIONNAIRES*

Name	Chamber	Party	Residence
Anderson, Thomas J.	House	D	Southgate
Angel, Dan	House	R	Marshall
Brennan, Bert C.	House	R	Saginaw
Bryant, William R., Jr.	House	R	Grosse Pointe Farms
Bullard, Perry	House	D	Ann Arbor
Crampton, Louis K.	House	R	Midland
De Stigter, Melvin	House	R	West Olive
Faust, William	Senate	D	Westland
Faxon, Jack	Senate	D	Detroit
Holmes, David S., Jr.	House	D	Detroit
McCollough, Patrick H.	Senate	D	Dearborn
Ostling, Ralph A.	House	R	Roscommon
Richardson, Robert	Senate	R	Saginaw
Strang, De Forrest	House	R	Sturgis
Thompson, Mark L.	House	R	Rogers City
Trezise, R. Douglas	House	R	Owosso
Wolpe, Howard	House	D	Kalamazoo
Ziegler, Hal W.	House	R	Jackson

*Five additional respondents did not sign their names to their questionnaires. One interviewee explained: "I don't know you. I don't know what you might do with the information (Watergate revisited!?).

APPENDIX C

ORAL QUESTIONNAIRE

I. General Role:

1. About how many hours do you put in during an average day? Could you break that down for me? That is, how much time is spent in committee, reading mail, etc.

2. Would you say that is typical of other legislators also?

3. What makes for an effective legislator? The number of bills he introduces? His work on committees? . . .

4. Is it important to master parliamentary procedures?

5. Do you have adequate staff assistance?

6. Are most of the important legislative assignments carried on by just a few legislators?

7. Have you noticed any significant changes in the legislature since reapportionment?

II. Personal Situation Before Nomination:

1. When did you become interested in politics?

2. Were you active then?

3. How did you become active?

4. What were some aspects of politics that you found interesting?

5. In making up your mind to run for the state legislature, what factors did you take into consideration?

6. Did the party play any role here?

7. Which single factor had the most to do with your final decision to seek office?

III. Campaign and Elections:

1. Was the party of any help in your campaign?

2. Did you get any outside help at all?

3. About how much did it cost to finance your campaign?

IV. Committee Work:

1. Which three committees are the most powerful? Why?

2. How expert and important are the committees? Why?

3. Do the committees have adequate research staffs?

4. Does the chairman have experience?

5. On what basis are bills assigned to committees? Who decides?

6. What are the mechanics for making committee appointments?

7. What are the decisive factors in gaining a committee assignment — expertise, party loyalty, etc.?

8. What role does the party leadership play in the assignment process?

9. Who chooses or decides who is committee chairman?

10. How important is seniority?

11. Do interest groups play a role in this process?

12. Does the Governor have a hand in this process?

13. What is the role of the committee chairman — written and unwritten?

14. What makes for an effective or powerful chairman?

15. Are there many subcommittees in the House/Senate?

16. Are subcommittees more important than the committees themselves?

17. How important is Committee Action on a Bill?

18. Are there any important select committees in the House/Senate? Which ones are they? Why?

19. About what percentage of the bills have to go into conference committees?

20. Who sits on the conference committees?

21. How important a role do public hearings play?

22. How would you say the members of the committees get along with one another?

23. How effective are the committees as a check on the executive branch? Could you give me an example?

24. Is there anything else about committees and their work that stands out in your mind?

V.   Party Leadership:

1. How would you describe the role played by political parties in the state legislature?

2. What are the differences between Republicans and Democrats in the state legislature?

3. Is there a distinction made between party men and independents (mavericks)? *If yes:*
   a) Under what circumstances is it not necessary to vote with your party?
   b) Is there any way in which the party can discipline mavericks? Has it ever happened?
   c) What are some of the advantages of going along with your party leaders when they seek your support on a bill? Anything else?

4. How much cooperation is there between the majority and minority leaders in the House/Senate?

5. Who are the most powerful people in the House/Senate? Why?

6. What role does the Governor play in the legislature?

VI. Interest Groups (Optional):

1. What are the most powerful interest groups in Michigan?

2. What particular organizations do you have in mind?

3. What are the main reasons for their influence?

4. I've been told that there are always some interest groups v'h)se advice ought to be considered whether they are powerful or not. Could you name some of these groups here in Michigan?

5. Could you tell me what there is about these groups that make them particularly worth listening to?

6. What are some of the techniques of interest groups which are effective? — ineffective?

VII. Leadership Roles in the Legislature:

1. What role ought the Speaker of the House (President Pro Tem) play in order to be most effective?

2. How close does he come to these expectations in general?

3. What role does the majority and/or minority leader play?

4. What is the role of the party whip?

5. Do the parties caucus? How often?

6. What is usually discussed in a caucus?

7. Do most of the important bills originate in the Governor's office?

VIII. Decision-Making:

1. How do you become informed about legislation which concerns an area in which you lack expertise?

2. How important a role does debate play in evaluating legislation?

3. Is debate important at all?

4. How effective is mail in influencing your decisions?

5. On what basis do you come to a decision as to how to vote?

IX. Miscellaneous:

1. What does the auditor general do for the legislators? Is he of much service?

2. What is the function of the Legislative Research Council?

3. Is it possible to talk a bill to death?

4. Does this, in fact, occur? How often?

5. How do the two chambers get along?

6. There are always conflicts in a legislature. How would you rank these particular conflicts:
   a) Republicans v Democrats
   b) Governor's supporters v his opponents
   c) cities v rural counties
   d) cities v suburbs
   e) liberals v conservatives
   f) labors friends v opponents of labor
   g) other (Please specify.)

7. Is there anything distinctive or unique about the Michigan state legislature that may not be true of other state legislatures?

8. What reforms or changes would you like to see brought about in the Michigan legislature?

9. Is there anything about the Michigan state legislature that you consider to be of significance and which we have failed to discuss?

Note: Not all of the foregoing questions were asked of all interviewees. Factors which determined which questions were discussed included the amount of time allotted for the interview, the responses of the particular legislator, the legislator's position and his length of service.

APPENDIX D

WRITTEN QUESTIONNAIRE

In the following questions, please indicate your choice by circling the appropriate response. Thank you.

Your name, please: _____

1. Why did you originally decide to run for office in the Michigan legislature?

   a. civic duty
   b. to further your political career
   c. financial reasons
   d. to effect change in the political system
   e. for the experience
   f. other (please specify):

2. Do you plan to run again in the Michigan legislature?

   a. Yes. If so, for the same office you now hold?
      i - yes
      ii - no
   b. No. If not, please state your reasons.

3. Was your party of any assistance in your last campaign?

   a. Yes (please specify).
   b. No.

4. Did your party play an important role in recruiting you to seek office in the legislature?

   a. Yes.
   b. No.

5. Does the state Democratic or Republican party play any role in the legislature?

   a. Yes. If so, what is this role?
   b. No.

6. What do you believe are the ideological differences between the Democratic and Republican parties here in Michigan?

7. What are your most important duties as a Michigan legislator?

8. Are you accomplishing the above objectives?

    a. Yes.
    b. No. Why not?

9. About what percentage of the time do you rely on each of the following in deciding how to vote?

    _____% a. other members of the legislature (including party leaders)
    _____% b. staff of, or assistants to, party leaders
    _____% c. committee staff
    _____% d. interest groups
    _____% e. other (please specify): _____

10. About how many hours in a typical working day are spent doing each of the following:

    _____ a. constituent relations (reading mail, greeting constituents, speaking to local groups, etc.)
    _____ b. attending committee sessions
    _____ c. attending floor sessions
    _____ d. reading, reviewing, and studying legislation.
    _____ e. meeting with representatives of interest groups
    _____ f. office management, directing the work of your staff.
    _____ g. other (please specify): _____

11. Is the Michigan state legislature effective in its oversight function in controlling executive agencies?

    a. Yes. Please give on example: _____
    b. No. Why not?

12. There are always conflicting opinions in a legislature. How would you rank these particular conflicts of opinion, in the order of their importance here in Michigan? (Number one is most important, number eight is least important.)

_____ a. Republican vs. Democrat
_____ b. liberal vs. conservative
_____ c. cities vs. rural counties
_____ d. Detroit vs. the rest of the state
_____ e. cities vs. suburbs
_____ f. the governor's supporters vs. his opponents
_____ g. labor's friends vs. opponents of labor
_____ h. other (please be specific): _____

13. Name the three committees which, in your opinion, are the most important in your branch of the legislature.

i - _____
ii - _____
iii - _____

14. Why are the above committees so important?

15. In your political campaign, did any interest group or groups assist you in any way?

a. Yes. Please identify these groups and describe the assistance they provided: _____
b. No.

16. Who are the three most effective and influential lobbies overall in the state legislature, and why? Please be specific, e.g. UAW, etc.

17. List the most important ways in which lobbyists or other advocates assist you.

18. What, if any, lobby activities by private interest groups or by the executive branch do you disapprove of most?

19. What role does the Governor play in the legislature?

20. In general, does the Michigan legislature have enough expertize to deal with the many and varied bills that come before it?

    a.   Yes.
    b.   No.
    Comments: _____

21. Name five (5) members of your branch (Senate/House) whom you consider to be subject matter experts in particular areas, and name those areas.

NAME   AREA OF EXPERTIZE

    a.
    b.
    c.
    d.
    e.

22. Name five (5) legislators in the Senate/House who do more than their share of the legislative load.

    a.
    b.
    c.
    d.
    e.

23. What reforms or changes would you like to see brought about in the Michigan state legislature?

24. If further information is needed, would you be agreeable to an in-person interview?

    a.   Yes.
    b.   No.

25. Have you any additional comments?

BIBLIOGRAPHY

Books

Adrian, Charles R. *State and Local Governments.* New York: McGraw-Hill Book Co., 1972.

Anton, Thomas J. *The Politics of State Expenditures in Illinois.* Urbana, Ill.: University of Illinois Press, 1966.

Baker, Gordon E. *Rural versus Urban Political Power.* New York: Doubleday & Co., Inc. 1955.

_____ . *The Reapportionment Revolution.* New York: Random House, Inc., 1966.

Bald, F. Clever. *Michigan in Four Centuries.* New York: Harper & Brothers, Publishers, 1954.

Barber, James D. *The Lawmakers: Recruitment and Adaptation to Legislative Life.* New Haven, Conn.: Yale University Press, 1965.

Carr, Robert W. *Government of Michigan Under the 1964 Constitution.* Ann Arbor, Mich.: University of Michigan Press, 1965.

Chester, Edward W. *Issues and Responses in State Political Experience.* New Jersey: Littlefield, Adams & Co., 1968.

Citizens Conference on State Legislatures. *The Sometime Governments.* New York: Bantam Books, Inc., 1971.

_____ . *State Legislatures: An Evaluation of Their Effectiveness.* New York: Praeger Publishers, 1971.

Council of State Governments. *The Book of the States.* 1964-1965, 1970-1971, and 1974-1975.

Crew, Robert E. *State Politics: Readings in Political Behavior.* Belmont, Calif.: Wadsworth Publishing Co., 1968.

Crotty, W.J., *et al.* (eds.). *Political Parties and Political Behavior.* Boston Allyn & Bacon, Inc., 1966.

Dixon, Robert G., Jr. *Democratic Representation: Reapportionment in Law and Politics.* New York: Oxford University Press, 1968.

Dunbar, Willis Frederick. *Michigan: A History of the Wolverine State.* Grand Rapids, Mich.: William B. Eerdman Publishing Co., 1970.

Dvorin, Eugene P., and Misner, Arthur J. *Governments Within the States.* Mass.: Addison-Wesley Publishing Co., 1971.

Dye, Thomas R. *Politics in States and Communities.* Englewood Cliffs, N.J.: Prentice-Hall, Inc., 1973.

_____ . *Politics, Economics, and the Public Policy Outcomes in the American States.* Chicago: Rand McNally & Co., 1966.

Ecker-Racz, L.I. *The Politics and Economics of State-Local Finance.* Englewood Cliffs, N.J.: Prentice-Hall, Inc., 1970.

Edinger, Lewis J. *Political Leadership in Industrialized Societies.* New York: John Wiley & Sons, Inc., 1967.

Elazar, Daniel. *American Federalism: A View From the States.* 2d ed. New York: Thomas Y. Crowell Co., 1972.

_____ . *Cities of the Prairie: The Metropolitan Frontier and American Politics.* New York: Basic Books, Inc., 1970.

Fenton, John F. *People and Parties in Politics.* Chicago: Scott, Foresman & Co., 1966.

Fischer, Floyd C. *The Government of Michigan.* Boston: Allyn & Bacon, Inc., 1965.

Formisano, Ronald P. *The Birth of Mass Political Parties: Michigan 1827-1861.* Princeton, N.J.: Princeton University Press, 1971.

Friedman, Robert S. *The Michigan Constitutional Convention and Administrative Organization: A Case Study in the Politics of Constitution Making.* Ann Arbor, Mich.: Institute of Public Administration, University of Michigan, 1963.

Fuller, Richard C. *George Romney and Michigan.* New York: Vantage Press, 1966.

Goldwin, Robert A. (ed.). *A Nation of States.* Chicago: Rand McNally & Co., 1963.

_____ (ed.). *Political Parties U.S.A.* Chicago: Rand McNally & Co., 1965.

Graves, W. Brooke. *American State Government.* 4th ed. Boston: D.C. Heath, 1953.

Grodzins, Morton. *The American System.* Chicago: Rand McNally & Co., 1966.

Hare, James M. *With Malice Toward None.* Lansing, Mich.: Michigan State University Press, 1972.

Heard, Alexander (ed.). *The American Legislative Process: Congress and the States.* Englewood Cliffs, N.J.: Prentice-Hall, Inc., 1968.

_____ . *State Legislatures in American Politics.* Englewood Cliffs, N.J.: Prentice-Hall, Inc., 1966.

Jacob, Herbert, and Vines, Kenneth N. (eds.). *Politics in the American States.* 2d ed. Boston: Little, Brown & Co., 1971.

Jewell, Malcolm E. *The State Legislature.* New York: Random House, Inc., 1962.

_____ and Patterson, Samuel C. *The Legislative Process in the United States.* New York: Random House, Inc., 1966.

Kaufman, Herbert. *Politics and Policies in State and Local Governments.* Englewood Cliffs, N.J.: Prentice-Hall, Inc., 1964.

Keefe, William J., and Ogul, Morris. *The American Legislative Process: Congress and the States.* Englewood Cliffs, N.J.: Prentice-Hall, Inc., 1968.

Kessler, James B. "Running for State Political Office," in Cornelius P. Cotter (ed.), *Practical Politics in the United States.* Boston: Allyn & Bacon, Inc., 1969. Pp. 119-141.

Key, Vladimar O., Jr. *American State Politics.* New York: Alfred A. Knopf, 1956.

_____ . *Political Parties and Pressure Groups.* 5th ed. New York: Thomas Y. Crowell Co., 1964.

La Palombara, Joseph. *Guide to Michigan Politics.* East Lansing, Mich.: Michigan State University Press, 1960.

Leach, Richard H. *American Federalism.* New York: W.W. Norton & Co., Inc., 1970.

Lewis, Ferris E. *State and Local Government in Michigan.* Hillsdale, Mich.: Hillsdale Educational Publishers, 1968.

Litt, Edgar. *The Political Culture of Massachusetts.* Cambridge, Mass.: The MIT Press, 1965.

Lockard, Duane. *The Politics of State and Local Government.* New York: The Macmillan Co., 1969.

Madge, John. *The Tools of Social Science.* Garden City. N.Y.: Doubleday & Co., Inc., 1965.

Matthews, Donald R. *U.S. Senators and Their World.* Chapel Hill, N.C.: University of North Carolina Press, 1960.

McConnell, Grant. *Private Power and American Democracy.* New York: Alfred A. Knopf, Inc., 1966.

Palmer, Kenneth T. *State Politics in the United States.* New York: St. Martin's Press, 1972.

Patterson, James T. *The New Deal and the States.* Princeton, N.J.: Princeton University Press, 1969.

Peirce, Neal R. *The Megastates of America.* New York: W.W. Norton & Co., Inc., 1972.

Pollock, James Kerr. *Making Michigan's New Constitution, 1961-1962.* Ann Arbor, Mich.: G. Wahr Publishing Co., 1962.

Ranney, Austin, and Kendall, Willmoore. *Democracy and the American Party System.* New York: Harcourt Brace Jovanovich, 1956.

Riker, William H. *The Study of Local Politics.* New York: Random House, 1959.

Rosenthal, Alan. *Legislative Performance in the States: Explorations of Committee Behavior*. New York: The Free Press, 1974.

Sanford, Terry. *Storm Over the States*. New York: McGraw-Hill Book Co., 1967.

Sarasohn, Stephen B. and Vera H. *Political Party Patterns in Michigan*. Detroit, Mich.: Wayne State University Press, 1957.

Sawyer, Robert Lee. *The Democratic State Central Committee in Michigan. 1949-1959: Rise of the New Politics and the New Political Leadership*. Ann Arbor, Mich.: Institute of Public Administration, University of Michigan, 1960.

Schick, Allen. *Budget Innovation in the States*. Washington, D.C.: The Brookings Institution, 1971.

Schlesinger, Joseph A. *Ambition and Politics: Political Careers in the United States*. Rand McNally & Co., 1966.

Seligman, Lester G. *Recruiting Political Elites*. New York: General Learning Press, 1971.

_____ et al. *Patterns of Recruitment: A State Chooses its Lawmakers*. Chicago: Rand McNally & Co., 1974.

Sharkansky, Ira. *The Maligned States*. New York: McGraw-Hill Book Co., 1972.

_____ . *Spending in the American States*. Chicago: Rand McNally & Co., 1968.

Sindler, Allan P. *Political Parties in the United States*. New York: St. Martin's Press, 1966.

Sorauf, Frank J. *Party and Representation*. New York: Atherton Press, 1963.

_____ . *Political Parties in the American System*. Boston: Little, Brown & Co., 1964.

Steiner, Gilbert Y., and Gore, Samuel. *Legislative Politics in Illinois*. Urbana, Ill.: University of Illinois Press, 1960.

Stieber, Carolyn. *The Politics of Change in Michigan.* Lansing, Michigan: Michigan State University Press, 1970.

Streeter, Floyd Benjamin. *Political Parties in Michigan.* Lansing, Mich.: Michigan Historical Commission, 1918.

Sturm, Albert L. *Constitution Making in Michigan, 1961-1962.* Ann Arbor, Mich.: Institute of Public Administration, University of Michigan, 1963.

_____. *Thirty Years of State Constitution Making, 1938-1968.* New York: National Municipal League, 1970.

Sundquist, James L. *Dynamics of the Party System.* Washington, D.C.: The Brookings Institution, 1973.

_____. *Making Federalism Work.* Washington, D.C.: The Brookings Institution, 1969.

Trippet, Frank. *The States: United They Fell.* New York: The World Publishing Co., 1967.

Truman, David B. *The Governmental Process.* New York: Alfred A. Knopf, Inc., 1965.

Wahlke, John C., *et al. The Legislative System.* New York: John Wiley & Sons, Inc., 1962.

Young, William H. *Ogg and Ray's Essentials of American State and Local Government.* 10th ed. New York: Appleton-Century-Crofts, 1969.

Zeigler, Harmon, and Baer, Michael. *Lobbying: Interaction and Influence in American State Legislatures.* Belmont, Calif.: Wadsworth Publishing Co., 1969.

Zeller, Belle. *American State Legislatures.* New York: Thomas Y. Crowell Co., 1954.

Articles and Periodicals

Becker, Robert W., et al. "Correlates of Legislative Voting: Michigan House of Representatives 1954-1961," *Midwest Journal of Political Science,* X (November, 1962), 384-96.

Bell, Roderick. "The Determinants of Psychological Involvement in Politics: A Casual Analysis," *Midwest Journal of Political Science,* XIII (May, 1969), 237-53.

Boynton, G.R., Patterson, Samuel, et al. "The Missing Links in Legislative Politics: Attentive Constituents," *Journal of Politics,* XXXI (August, 1969), 700-21.

"Campaign '72: Michigan Presidential Primary," *Congressional Quarterly,* XXX, No. 19 (May 6, 1972), 1032.

Cnudde, Charles F., and McCrone, Donald J. "Party Competition and Welfare Policies in the American States," *American Political Science Review,* LXIII (September, 1969), 858-66.

Crane, Wilder W., Jr. "Do Representatives Represent?" *Journal of Politics,* XXII (May, 1960), 295-99.

Crittenden, John. "Dimensions of Modernization in the American States," *American Political Science Review,* LXI (December, 1967), 335-40.

Dawson, Richard E., and Robinson, James A. "Inter-Party Competition, Economic Variables and Welfare Policies in the American States," *Journal of Politics,* XXV (May, 1963), 265-89.

Derge, David R. "The Lawyer as Decision-Maker in the American State Legislature," *Journal of Politics,* XXI (August, 1959), 408-33.

Dye, Thomas R. "Income Inequality and American State Politics," *American Political Science Review,* LXIII (March, 1969), 157-63.

_____ . "Malapportionment and Public Policy in the States," *Journal of Politics,* XXVII (August, 1965), 586-601.

Erikson, Robert S. "The Partisan Impact of State Legislative Reapportionment," *Midwest Journal of Political Science,* XV (February, 1971), 57-71.

_____ . "The Relationship Between Party Control and Civil Rights Legislation in the American States," *Western Political Quarterly*, XXIV (March, 1971), 1978-82.

Eulau, Heinz, *et al.* "The Political Socialization of American State Legislatures," *Midwest Journal of Political Science*, III (May, 1959), 188-206.

Fenton, John H., and Chamberlayne, Donald W. "The Literature Dealing With the Relationship Between Political Processes, Socio-Economic Conditions, and Public Policies in the American States," *Polity 1*, (Spring, 1969), 388-404.

Fiellin, Alan. "The Functions of Informal Groups in Legislative Institutions: A Case Study," *Journal of Politics*, XXIV (1962), 72-91.

Flinn, Thomas A. "Party Responsibility in the States: Some Causal Factors," *American Political Science Review*, LVIII (March, 1964), 60-71.

Francis, Wayne L. "Influence and Interaction in a State Legislative Body," *American Political Science Review*, LVI (December, 1962), 953-60.

Frederickson, H. George, and Cho, Yong Hyo. "Legislative Apportionment and Fiscal Policy in the American States." *Western Political Quarterly*, XXVII (March, 1974), 5-38.

Friedman, Robert S. "The Urban-Rural Conflict Revisited" *Western Political Quarterly*, XIV (June, 1961), 481-95.

Froman, Lewis A., Jr. "Some Effects of Interest Group Strength in State Politics," *American Political Science Review*, LX (December, 1966), 952-62.

Fry, Brian R., and Winters, Richard F. "The Politics of Redistribution," *American Political Science Review*, LXIV (June, 1970), 508-22.

Grumm, John G. "A Factor Analysis of Legislative Behavior," *Midwest Journal of Political Science*, VII (November, 1963), 336-56.

Hanson, Roger A., and Crew, Robert E. "The Policy Impact of Reapportionment," *Law and Society Review*, VIII (Fall, 1973), 69-75.

Hofferbert, Richard I. "Classification of American State Party Systems," *Journal of Politics*, XXVI (August, 1964), 550-67.

Hyneman, Charles. "Who Makes Our Laws?" *Political Science Quarterly*, LV (1940), 556-81.

Jacob, Herbert. "Initial Recruitment of Elected Officials in the U.S.: A Model," *Journal of Politics*, XXIV (November, 1962), 703-16.

_____ , and Lipsky, Michael. "Outputs, Structure and Power: An Assessment of Changes in the Study of State and Local Politics," *Journal of Politics*, XXX (May, 1968), 510-38.

Jennings, M. Kent, and Zeigler, Harmon. "The Salience of American State Politics," *American Political Science Review*, LXIV (June, 1970), 523-35.

Jewell, Malcolm E. "Party Voting in American State Legislatures," *American Political Science Review*, XLIX (1955), 773-91.

Jones, Bryan D. "Competitiveness, Role Orientation and Legislative Responsiveness," *Journal of Politics*, XXXV (November, 1973), 924-47.

Key, Vladimar O., Jr. "The Direct Primary and Party Structure: A Study of State Legislature Nominations," *American Political Science Review*, XLVIII (March, 1954), 1-26.

Kirkpatrick, Evron M. "Toward a More Responsible Two-Party System: Political Science, Policy Science, or Pseudo-Science?" *American Political Science Review*, LXV (December, 1971), 965-90.

Kolasa, Bernard D. "Lobbying in the Nonpartisan Environment: The Case of Nebraska," *Western Political Quarterly*, XXIV (March, 1971), 65-78.

Kurfess, Charles F. "State Legislatures: A Record of Accomplishment," *State Government*, XLVII (Autumn, 1974), 247-52.

Longley, Lawrence D. "Interest Group Interaction in a Legislative System," *Journal of Politics*, XXIV (August, 1967), 637-58.

Macrae, Duncan, Jr. "The Role of the State Legislator in Massachusetts," *American Sociological Review*, XIX (1954), 185-94.

Meller, Norman. "Legislative Staff Services: Toxin, Specific or Placebo for the Legislature's Ills," *Western Political Quarterly*, XX (June, 1967), 381-9.

"Michigan Primary Results," *Congressional Quarterly*, XXX, No. 21 (may 20, 1972), 1139.

Monsma, Stephen V. "Interpersonal Relations in the Legislative System: A Study of the 1964 Michigan House of Representatives," *Midwest Journal of Political Science*, VI (August, 1966), 350-63.

Morehouse, Sarah M. "The State Political Party and the Policy-Making Process," *American Political Science Review*, LXVII (March, 1973), 55-72.

Parker, John D. "Classifications of Candidate Motivations for First Seeking Office," *Journal of Politics*, XXIV (February, 1972), 268-71.

Patterson, Samuel C. "The Political Culture of the American States," *Journal of Politics*, XXX (February, 1968), 187-209.

_____ . "Legislative Leadership and Political Ideology," *Public Opinion Quarterly*, XXVII (Fall, 1963), 399-410.

Prewitt, Kenneth. "Political Ambitions, Volunteerism, and Electoral Accountability," *American Political Science Review*, LXIV (March, 1970), 5-18.

Ray, David. "Membership Stability in Three State Legislatures, 1893-1969," *American Political Science Review*, LXVIII (March, 1974), 106-112.

Riley, Dennis D. "Party Competition and State Policy Making: The Need for a Re-Examination," *Western Political Quarterly*, XXIV (September, 1971), 510-13.

Ritt, Leonard G. "State Legislative Reform: Does it Matter?" *American Politics Quarterly*, I, No. 4 (1971), 499-511.

Rosen, Corey. "Legislative Influence and Policy Orientation in American State Legislatures," *American Journal of Political Science*, XVIII (November, 1943), 681-693.

Rosenthal, Alan. "An Analysis of Institutional Effects: Staffing Legislative Parties in Wisconsin," *Journal of Politics,* XXXII (August, 1970), 531-62.

_____ . "Turnover in State Legislatures," *American Journal of Political Science,* XVIII (August, 1974), 609-16.

Seligman, Lester G. "Political Recruitment and Party Structure: A Case Study," *American Political Science Review,* LV (March, 1961), 77-86.

Sharkansky, Ira. "The Utility of Elazar's Political Culture: A Research Note," *Polity 2,* (Fall, 1969), 81.

_____ , and Hofferbert, Richard. "Dimensions of State Politics, Economics, and Public Policy," *American Political Science Review,* LXIII (September, 1969), 867-79.

Sokolow, Alvin D., and Brandsma, Richard W. "Partisanship and Seniority in Legislative Committee Assignments: California After Reapportionment," *Western Political Quarterly,* IV (December, 1971), 740-60.

Soule, John W. "Future Political Ambitions and the Behavior of Incumbent State Legislators," *Midwest Journal of Political Science,* XIII (August, 1969), 439-454.

Teune, Henry. "Legislative Attitudes Toward Interest Groups," *Midwest Journal of Political Science,* XI (November, 1967), 489-504.

Wahle, John C., *et al.* "American State Legislators' Role Orientation Toward Pressure Groups," *Journal of Politics,* XXII (February, 1960), 203-27.

Walker, Jack L. "The Diffusion of Innovations Among the American States," *American Political Science Review,* LXIII (September, 1969), 880-99.

Wellhofer, Spender, and Hennessey, Timothy M. "Political Party Development: Institutionalization, Leadership, Recruitment and Behavior," *American Journal of Political Science,* XVIII (February, 1974), 135-65.

Wilson, James Q. "Corruption: The Shame of the States," *Public Interest,* II (Winter, 1966), 28-38.

Other Sources

Citizens Advisory Committee. *Michigan Constitutional Convention.* A Report Prepared for the Governor of Michigan, John B. Swainson, by the Legislative Department. September, 1961.

Detroit Free Press. October & November, 1962, 1972-74.

Detroit News. 1972-74.

Gongwers News Service.

"Michigan," *Encyclopaedia Britannica,* 14th ed. XV (1968), 373-75.

_____ , 15th ed. Macropaedia, XII (1974), 104-9.

State of Michigan. *Michigan Manual.* The Department of Administration. 1961-1962, 1971-1972, and 1973-1974.

U.S. Bureau of the Census. *Nineteenth Census of the United States: 1970. Population.*